The Core Truth Of It All

What you feel and what's real are two different things

Poem Book by **Latausha Bonner**

Latausha Bonner

Contents

Dedication

This book is dedicated to the women who are actually in love and is feeling their mate, to the women in a "relationship" but is not sure what to call it, to the women who have fallen out of love because of the lies and the cheating from their ex or current mate.

There are other women out there who know exactly what you are going through. Understand and know that no, you are not tripping, you are not confused, this is not the end, this is just the beginning, and you are not broken.

Just take a moment to clear your mind, understand your worth and know when to move on. Life is way too short to live with stress and regret. You know what you want and you know exactly what you need. Take that and run with it. Go for what you want.

YOU ARE THE PRIZE

Also, this book is dedicated to any women who did not ignore the way she felt and stood up and said what was on her mind, took action, and did not look back. To the women who actually know their power and refuse to let anyone take their power away from them.

Do not ignore the way you feel to make someone else happy or because you are scared someone else will take your someone else.

People will treat you how you allow them to treat you. Letting someone else control your life is giving away your power. Putting your foot down will get you what you want. You are special and you are unique, do not let anyone downplay you into thinking you are anything less than that.

TAKE BACK YOUR POWER YOU DESERVE IT

To the person that has a dream so big only they can see it. DO NOT let other people's opinions about your dream stop you, discourage you, or the fear of wanting more hold you back. Set goals, change your way of thinking, and take action. The world is yours to do what you want with it.

IF YOUR DREAMS DON'T SCARE YOU THEN YOU ARE NOT DREAMING BIG ENOUGH

Introduction

I am very humbled and would like to thank you for even being interested in reading my poetry. I feel poetry is a way of expressing myself in a strong short way. The effect a couple of words can have on people's lives is amazing.

Throughout the years I have noticed how I deal with men and why I have not been successful with men, to be honest. I had to really take a step back from myself and question myself like "Is it me or is it them?" My honest answer was it was me. I was not trying hard to please any man I ever dealt with, I became too easy and obedient when it came to men, and was having relations with men but found myself single. For those reasons, I wrote this poetry book "The Core Truth of it all", because I know I am not the only woman beating myself up about men and why things never work out.

I write to empower you, to have you think from another perspective, and to have you step outside of yourself and maybe change something in your life that is not giving you a positive outcome. I have always loved to empower women. Confidence is everything, believing in yourself, and knowing your worth is very important in life. Confidence will help when finding your soul mate or even reaching your dreams.

It was very important for me to write these poems to make women laugh, cry, and also to understand that one bad relationship does not mean all men are the same. It also does not mean your relationship in the future will be negative or not turn out for the better.

People's attitudes towards whatever you are trying to do should not stop you, but it should motivate you and make you want it even more.

Stay positive and surround yourself with positive people

People need to know where they stand in other people's lives. Many people cannot communicate how they really feel, so it is up to the person who really wants something out of the relationship to speak up. Speak on what is really important to you. If the other person does not want a relationship and you do then you have a choice to make, sit around and wait for that person or move on. It sounds simple because it is.

There are so many people that are afraid of being alone. There is absolutely nothing wrong with being alone. Find yourself and what really makes you happy. No one else will do this for you. Sometimes you have to be selfish for you.

The encouragement, advice, and life-changing information I have already given women are proof my information you're about to read is motivational and will inspire you to do better, demand more, and think positive about yourself.

Read to the end because there are questions I am sure you will have to think about to get an honest answer out of yourself.

What you demand is what you get!

Strength

Blind

In

Love

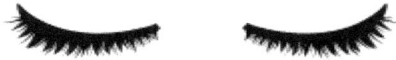

Chapter One

LOVE IS BLIND

Cement Love

I want that real love
That no question about it love
That he knows me and I know him
No question about us love
That he got my back love
That even when I'm wrong I'm right love
That laid-back cool we alright love
That incredible love
That he sees no other female and not looking in the rear
view mirror love
That he only wants me love
We got our own world love
That patient love
That loyal we see eye to eye love
We here love

Not gazing around love
Will fight for this love
Yes that respectful you got me love
Much like written in the ground cement love
That no one else can have or change this love

Fire

Sheets go for miles

Hands shaking crying out for the forgiveness of everything our
eyes missed

Dark clouds never shine

So in a locked house in the back room only made sense

Hold tight I rather wait than to bypass a glimpse

Caught a glimpse and couldn't sit still

Back and forth was all worth the wait

Goosebumps and shivers

Looking at me but through me

Thoughts that will be forgotten

Only in our dreams, they will be brought in

His weight like stones being thrown skipping over a lake going
nowhere but sinking somewhere to the back of that last stroke

This dude chased the fire, locked it down, and told me no
one else like I had no choice and he had the choice to choose to tap
or nap

No joke he handcuffed me and whispered in my ear trust me

The whole time I'm taking the side of insecure because the lights
were on and his eyes examined pulling back every

confident strand I had in me

The lines and dots he saw was not a surprise
A grown woman with fire all in before I could ask a
question or even realized I was all he desired

Second Place

Why do women put themselves in second place

Like winning that is first place in a race
Sometimes it's written all over their face
But they have to face the fact they put themselves number
two in the running race
Hey
Feel like I'm running a race
But to all women, there is no comparison and should not be
hard to replace
I act like I'm letting shit ride
When in reality it's hard to let it slide
Seem like the one you want is not available
Seem like the one you want is not replaceable
Damn he so embraceable
His love is inescapable
Even though our situation is unbreakable
But this one I should spare
Too many women in a running race
Taking second place
Know your worth

Every woman deserves gold
She should come first and never second place

Afternoon Tea

Your love is like afternoon tea

Hot and sweet

I got a crush on your kisses

Boy I used to be obsessed with those faces

Don't you know I love you to pieces

Spots I could tell you are too delicious

That loving so damn vicious

Being this deep in love might be considered armed and

dangerous

But don't hesitate

I love the dang in us

The change in us

The phase in us

And the faith in us

Hot damn

Out of body experience Goddamn

Hot tea

You and me

Enjoying each others company

Living carefree

Die

Don't die for me just live for me I lost enough in my lifetime so
please just breathe for me

Don't die for me just live with me

We all go through things I need you to survive for me

Don't die for me please pray for me

No one is perfect be patient and have much respect for me

Don't need you to die for me just be there for me

I am not difficult hope my words don't come off as an insult

Do not die for me fight you're all with me

One person is strong but with two we can never go wrong

Don't die for me choose to walk down all the right roads with me

No own lane left lane or a major change

The straight lane, focused lane, the one that will drive us in
love and even insane

One last time please do not die for me all I want is for you
to make love to me

Latausha Bonner

Fight

I once heard that you should not fight for what you had but to fight
for much more

More love

More truth

More realness

More you

More of self

More them

Much more for your kids

Much more between us

I also heard people will fight for the love they think they deserve

People want their old thing back

As long as they have someone to call their own

So what are you really fighting for

And will it be much worth you being alone

Things to fight for in your life are?

_____

_____

18

Good Old Feeling

That good old feeling will make you forget about the world and the people in it

That feeling that will have you speechless and could put any human being through it

That feeling will make you so consumed having you not knowing what to do

"I cannot protect myself so we can go without"

"I don't care what you put in me but we will figure it out"

"Hurry up so I can get back to my family" It's what she screams out loud

Cause this feeling will make you feel not a care in the world

Have you sneaking out and running about

Got you out here like a wild animal

That good old feeling will have your ass settling

Have your ass crying, fighting, and arguing

That good old feeling they say is better than drugs

That good old feeling is the result of deaths, betrayals, and breakups

Boy will have you lying and spying

Becoming friends with the enemy

Even spreading lies

Becoming involved with your best friends girl

Or loving a married man
Well is it all worth that feeling
Very powerful
Just tell me what you do
With so much guilt never knew
Or had a clue of what you would ever do

You

I like your style though
No problems and your smile though
I like your wild though
Your loving and your wild flow
I love your toughness
Love making and your roughness
I love your thoroughness
Mind blowing and your realness
The talks though
Conversations and your walk though
Misunderstood though
Mean mugging gives me chills though
Might have a past though
Living life on the fast go
I got a real flow
Can't stop
Won't stop
It's way too real though
And one no one will ever know

Latausha Bonner

Journey Called Love

Let's walk

No, let's run

Cause being in love with you is so much fun

From your eyes to your lips to your smile

You bring me so much pride

Pride pride pride

Let's ride

No...no let's walk

I mean run

I'm so excited about the things that are to come

The way you hold my hand

To the way you look me in my eyes

Boy you so fine

Let's fly

No, let's walk

Dang I mean run

Run into each other

Run into love

This journey called love could last forever as long as you ready
and willing to love me way better

Water

Don't be the female that gives him a hard time
Enjoy the time feel him out have good vibes
No one wants to be around the female that nags
He wants a female around him so he can brag
Have fun sometimes go with the flow
Especially once you see he's all about you why be a
headache and a no-show
Too many poisonous toxins walking around
Love being the talk of the town
Unhealthy, unnatural, and unsafe
Stay away so you can live many years and keep your heart safe
Clean, purified, and fresh
Do all you can to be his best
Refresh his mind and restore his body
Be more than just that somebody
Be his everybody
Now that is how you love and take care of a man's body

Bittersweet

Kiss me so I know it's real

Touch me so I can heal

Speak truth so I know the deal

Let's chill to reveal

Never hesitate for anyone to steal

Becoming all about us creating surreal

Speak on our opportunities

Unbelievable who's standing next to me

My body when I'm weak

My sunshine so I can see

Blood flowing through me so strong

Relate so I know we belong

Stand for me a man powerful and headstrong

The little things are what I live for

Cannot wait impatient and all over the place

This dude is too surreal

Can't stop searching

My thoughts and what's real are bittersweet

The uncommitted, unloved, and unwilling is what keeps bumping
into me

But waiting and cannot wait to meet

Reach For Love

Don't let him slip away from your arms
Keep him real close to your heart
Don't let him run away
Let him know he is the one you want to stay
Don't let him go too far from your heart
Because he just might find another heart
Be real and tell him how you feel
Because if you don't he will find someone who will
Don't be too quick to tell him he is wrong
Because it will not be long before he walks out the door
Be sure your love is forever and ever
And if it's not change something to make it better
Tell him he is right when he is wrong
Tell him you love him when you hate him
Tell him yes when you want to say no
Just to keep him close
Say whatever you have to say to keep him within arms reach
But if he is not
Reach for love

Some Business

We got some business to handle and this cannot wait
See I been waiting a long time to talk to you
I am excited hopefully not but I might be a little late
I was a little shy to talk to you about it
But this feeling is getting worse and I cannot shake it
Come here sit down and try to understand
I'm going to be a woman about it so please be a man
Show me you understand if you do take my
hand
Show me you comprehend by looking me in my eyes
I am not going to lie this business right
here is between you and me
Outside of this no one should know and I promise we
will grow

Blow

Blow my mind
Cross the line
Explode inside of me
Grip me up
Rough me up
Slap me down
Put on a show
Clown around
Put pressure on me
Impressed
Press upon me
Back flips
Lift this
Twist this
Bend this
I'm all in
Blow my mind
Get behind
Blow my mind
Unwind
Act a fool

Latausha Bonner

Tonight there are no rules

Scream my name

Say it again

You came

Came to play no games

Hot and sticky

Those positions were tricky

Wet and warm

You showed out and you performed

Blow my mind

I promise you I won't mind

Just Enough part 1

Mariah said she wanted her body touched

But you looking at me I say that's just enough

I see why you like what you see

And me being taken makes you want me more I can see

Confuses the hell out of me that the more I push you pull

You say whatever comes to your mind no matter if it makes

you look a damn fool

You wish you were in my life

But as friends, we not doing alright

So anything more would cause fights and stay up late nights

But you see I want to spend none of your money or drive none of

your cars

Just a kiss, a hug, and your time is just enough

Latausha Bonner

Backbone

Can he give me his all

Will he pick me up when I fall

Will he love me forever

Can he run to me whenever

When I feel like I want to cry

Down and out and want to die

When it's that time of the month

And I put on a front

Will he understand and still be only my man

Will he take my side even when I'm wrong then at home

when all doors are closed give the truth soft and not strong

Will he give it to me real

Steal my heart and make me feel like the only woman in his life

When I cry will he smile

When I'm weak can he be strong

And when I feel like I have nothing will he give me everything

Can this dude be my backbone or out of fear will I have to leave
this dude alone

Like myself, most women give more then what they are getting.
Never give too much to someone and let them make you feel like
they are draining the life out of you. What you want matters too!

Self Love Much Like A Queen

It's easier to love someone else

Make excuses instead of loving one's self

Especially when you get lonely and want love so you go for
anyone you see

It really does not matter if he has a woman and married with
children

As long as he comes over to show you he is willing

A lot of women want to feel love and get love

So they do whatever

Stumble upon whomever

And will do it whenever where ever

Self-love

Self-respect

It comes from inside and will show out

Show them dudes you're hard to get

Let them know from the beginning it's going to take more than

delicious words whispered in your ear and him

buying you a drink

Just think about it

You're worth

I am worthy

Latausha Bonner

So much more
No matter who you like or have been with
Always want more for you
It's crazy because I been through it
Had to learn it myself by myself
Try to resemble a queen with much more respect
Who also love one's self
You are a queen
And believe me a man's dream

Hello part 1

Hello to the one and only I love

Hello to the one I will always put above

Hello to that sweet and kind gentleman

The one I know will treat me like a real woman

Hello you fine and sexy thing

I will be more than happy to be your wife so give me that
wedding ring

Hey you must be God's greatest creation

You are an amazing human being

Seeing you makes me happy

Yes it brings me joy

Words cannot describe how you make me feel

Hello to the most beautiful, cutest, the most wonderful man
in the world

Hello!

Walk over here my one and only true love

Since Hello part 2

Kinda Perfect

Perfect man, we made some plans

Spent some time

Went a few places

Made some lovemaking

You know how it goes

Said some words did not talk for a few hours

One of those break up to make up love things going on

Arguing over the phone

But I know how he really feels

My man will always come back home for this good

Ashanti said

Said he never felt this way

And I was the best

Better than the rest

And I come first cannot ever mess with no one less

That all sounded good

He cooked and brought gifts

Said he was falling in love

And would never put anyone else above

Broke The Rules

You have to give it time

Give you two some time to vibe

Even when your hormones be racing

When your body wants it but your heart does not sit back
and face it

Because you know he wants it

Saying no will give you time to think about it

But saying yes you just might have some things to rethink
about it

There is no rush

Tell him to hush and get out your ear

All he wants is for you to give it up, steal your heart, and
corrupt your mind

Find a way out cause in a minute it will be too late

Too late to walk away because your living on cloud nine

Too late to say no because before he asked he already had
his mind made up about you

Don't break the rules and tell him yes

Make him work

Because you know your worth

Make his ass wait

Stop Lying

There is nothing wrong with having a man

One who sticks by your side and also one who understands

Why you in denial

You acting like you on trial

Oh word, you that good

So you don't get lonely sometimes

Well in your situation I damn for sure would

You never dreamed of a man much like Robin Hood

Girl stop lying I know you don't mind him staying

I mean I'm just saying you displaying shit in the open like you don't appreciate that man

So it goes without saying you happy where you at

Well how about that

I never knew

After all, you two have been through

But no, tell me what the real issue is

Because you in denial and lying about way too much

So you don't like his touch

Girl, I think you running out of luck

Think you better get in touch with the real world

Because you living in a dream world

And nowadays females taking men like yours

Best put a hold on him before you become like one of them
wishing you had a man

Women these days are too hard. Become sensitive and fragile
again. It's okay to need the opposite sex. We are human beings.

Latausha Bonner

Stop Tripping

Maybe I don't trip because I know what I got

Maybe I don't trip because I know I'm a keeper for real

Maybe I don't trip because I know I am a queen

Maybe I don't trip because I know he looking for me

Maybe I don't trip because I got patience but feel I don't for real

Maybe I don't trip because I already got me

Maybe I don't trip because with or without I'm good

Maybe I don't trip because I've been blessed with my three beautiful children

Maybe I don't trip because at the end of the day I know me for real

Get to know YOU. Do not trip because you are running out of patience and think you are running out of time. Timing is everything. Just because you want something to happen for you right away it just may not be your time. God is on your side and at the right time, he will give you everything you are searching for. You also must believe. SO STOP TRIPPING

Teacher

Who is your teacher I would love to meet her
Who taught you how to kiss
Rub me down and french kiss this
Going at this
Boy who does this
Wait wait
First, let's reminisce
Because I missed this
Who is your teacher
I would love to meet her
Who taught you how to hug
To spread me out and start to rub
I don't have any strength
Why you want me weak in the knees
This is too intense
Don't make a bit of Goddamn sense
Feeling like I have to put up my defense
But also love the suspense
Please who is your teacher
I would like to meet her
The sex the love the attention

Latausha Bonner

Just wanted to mention
Don't want to close my eyes
A nightmare I might be dreaming
And too much apprehension
Spoil me touch me talk to me
You know just how to put me at ease
You squeeze and make me drop to my knees
That teacher of yours got skills
I would love to meet her

Say

How

You

Feel

Believe in speaking your mind

Chapter Two

In Between/Confused

Broken

Broken

Heart Broken

Soft-spoken

You need confidence home girl

Find your own

Get in your zone

You too grown

Too beautiful

Too smart

To be all alone

Broken in

Out broken

Unbroken

Defines the real you

I'm so surprised you just don't do you

See through all the pettiness

Take it for what it is

Don't live in no fantasy world because things will only be okay
once you admit that you are not okay

Stop being these weak dudes prey

They gone play

They gone downplay

Stop giving them so much leeway

You're better than that

Stop being a doormat

Your not broken

Just too damn soft spoken

Where is the power you once gave away

Find it, accept it, live with it

You say you're broken

I say I'm lucky

You say you stressed

I say I'm blessed

You say you're sad

I say I'm glad

You say negative all over you

I say positive things pouring out of me

You say you have no more options

Latausha Bonner

I say the world is my option
You say they take advantage
I say I am the advantage
You say you were fooled
I say I played the fool
You say you were blind
I say keep your eyes wide open
You misunderstood
I understand and over stand
You cry
I sing
You scream
I praise
Girl you not broken
You just too damn soft spoken

Dedication

To the girl standing around at the after party pretending to be waiting on someone but really is waiting for someone

A lot of love built up

Just want someone who can build her up

A dry phone too many men known but still finds herself alone

Always let down

Partying at the wrong places no good men just a big let down

Job after job no good luck

Annoyed with it all and says it's her bad luck

Overwhelmed

Giving up easily speak slowly I know your listening

Pretty insecure

Pretty and insecure

Hesitate

No need to wait you can eat and have your cake

Looks good does not mean he is good, meaning good, meanwhile hustling for a dollar minding his own business in the hood

Kids holding her back

Remember the love you have for them should never make

Latausha Bonner

you slack

A diamond in the ruff

Too different she feels the feeling and comes off mad tough

The mindset and knowledge of historians

For this reason, it's hard to let someone in

A heart of gold but it's solid amazed by how no one can break it or

mold it

A passion but too scared so, work a workaholic

Manage to strive through working hard will get you through

No pride being humble will help get you through

A focused mind dedication and love will move you through

Stay fair because people like that are very rare

A Professional

It hurts me that I hurt you

I try to love you but love not strong enough to move me

I feel the passion but stay looking past it

I see our forever but good luck mine is never

I'm a pro at what I do

I like but won't hesitate to dislike

I see the stars in your eyes

But the universe itself telling you she is not me

Just buy me things and leave me

Just sex me then disrespect me

Cause I'm a pro at what I do

And who's to say what day and time I will grow

Day by day hurt looking for my king

But my actions show me you're not ready

Messing with these bums who swear they doing things

God himself know I'm a pro at what I do

Waste time

Wasted enough time

Feel in like never feel in love

A mindset of a man

Latausha Bonner

But no much like these dudes cause I don't respect

I don't love them

I could care less about them

Sitting here butt naked

Smelling fresh

Can't wait for someone to undress me

Undressing me

These layers of skin so disrespectful to my flesh

Please just let me rest

Never knew me much like I know me today

Hard on me but one day a true king will come along and really just

want me

Busy

I see the frustration

Because you are getting impatient

He says he is real because he told you from the beginning

So why you all in your feelings like "How could he I should
be the main woman"

You tend to hide your hurt because this dude cannot explain
what he already told you

So why can't you come outside it's going over and over in
your head girl I already told you why

You're angry

But the reason you're giving me does not add up you see

Your headaches are coming from your heartache

You're nervous

It's because he moves weird just curious

You let yourself go

Because this dude stay on the go

From me to you a real man will never let you go

And if he does he will explain why you should not take it
personal

This dude is not busy because of kids and work

He busy because from the start he never wanted to make it work

Hip

A lot of dudes know some women don't know any better
So they challenge our mindset hoping we're not clever
They literally sit there while women walk around like zombies
Like she screaming for help save her she crying
I only have one wish for women to open their eyes
But I know shit way deeper than me inspiring
A world filled with dudes that swear women are not hip
So I challenge you
One tip abandon ship
It's not your fault and no you're not dumb
Everyone moves on their own time but you deserve respect
Go out and get you some
You know something is missing
So why not go get it
Get hip to respect
Hip to "Baby why you so upset"
Hip to a lifetime of happiness
Thank God I'm so happy you're reading this
Hip to gratitude
Less of an attitude
And I promise you he only sees you

Get hip to appreciation
Loving yourself I forgot to mention
Girl, you slipped upon the wrong guy it's okay it wasn't your time
Just get hip to their lifestyle

Home Remedy

Nowadays there are home remedies for everything
But no home remedy for a broken heart
Nowadays they just say you should have been smart
But I love from the heart and it blocked the true person he
is
Held me back from seeing his sins
And guarded me against the real
Get this
The dark cloud above his head and demon in him I refused to see
I rather him loving on me than to have seen anything supernatural
laying upon me
True colors uncovered
Knew I should have taken cover
But my name coming out his voice sang mountains in the storming
rain
Pain just didn't cut deep enough
So walking around with blood dripping from my heart was
the only way I knew we would remain
On top of that making sure I don't leave any bloodstains
Since there are no home remedies I'll just patch it up and deal
No worries I know for a fact I will heal

I'm tough but had enough of dealing with this pain

Opposite Lovers

Why grow together then fall apart

Accept what is going on

To get upset to leave exit to the right

So far apart

Why say it will last forever

When in the back of your mind you know damn well never

Why try to prove with words

When you know actions don't show and soon hurt

Why miss me

And at the same time say it's not me

What is your agenda

Go move to the side so I can see and hear what is more real

Why cry them fake crocodile tears

When me being with another man is what you really fear

Why treat me like a queen now

When you had years but all you did was embarrass me

A couple minutes ago you were acting real hard

Now you feeling soft because now your whole world falling

apart

I don't know what to tell you

When for years you had stories but lies are what you choose to tell

me

Better grow up now because a weak insecure guy is who I can
never settle for now

Feelings VS Reality

Special feelings will eventually need years of healing

Into deep is so powerful

You could eventually hate yourself

No respect

Down and out

Upset

Will leave years of much doubt

Regret haunts you

Neglect loves you

Hate spoils you

You have lost the real you

Feelings got you all lost

Got you feeling like you gave it all away at no cost

Then reality hit

He did not want the real you

All he wanted to do was feel you

Feeling him feeling you

He did not love your conversations

All he wanted to do was chill be just another guy and have

you stick around no matter the situation

Leave your feelings at the door when dealing with men. What do you really want a relationship or just a situation? With most females, feelings will win over what is really going on. You have control over your world. Why live in a fantasy world when you know what really is going on?

Worthy

Sometimes you can be too good for someone

Their insecurities all over the place

Because they know they will never amount to what you deserve

You deserve the earth, the moon, and the stars

Cliche

But no, you deserve someone who keeps their promises, buys you

flowers, and actually don't pull off until your in the house

Fantasy

No reality

Because chicks are getting what they deserve

And the man that says he loves her actually proves he loves her
and worships the ground she walks on

Doing too much

No your man or the dude you call a man not doing enough

That's why you question every time he walks out the door

That's exactly why you question when he doesn't answer the phone

I got some advice

Without a doubt

This man not on your level

Or is he and is that the reason you accept it

Substitute

In need of a substitute because you acting brand new

But from start knew it wasn't you

Should have paid more attention

Inside knew I was losing you

I don't know what happened

Inside still know I got it

The last thing I heard was a text

A phone call is what I would have preferred

Knew my walls were up for a reason

Getting to know you for what

For no reason

Pain go away

It's okay I still pray

A wonderful woman I am

So I don't know why I'm questioning my strengths

Glad I never bend over backward

Cause it took a second for you to run back to her

Remembering who I really am

So now I am looking for a substitute someone like a friend

Latausha Bonner

Far Away

What if I say I don't love you anymore

Would you cry try to change my mind

What if I say I don't care I'm leaving

Would you get in my way try to hold me back and get me to stay

Or would you go on your way and say I don't care either

Anyways we should not be together

Either of us should be together

At one time you said we would be together forever

I should of never ever listened to you

Should I stay say okay

Should I go far away

I could stay maybe then I'll say okay

But for right now my mind is not made up

Even though I'm upset I want to stay

My mind tells me to go I'm halfway out the door

But my heart says stay

Even though I want to be on my way

But I'm here with you even though I want to fly far far

away

Get Away

First, you heard I wanted to fly away
Now I want to get away
Wish I had money for a getaway
As a matter, a fact just get away
I do not want this back and forth
How about you go south while I go north
Two different directions
Away from you and your obsessions
Boy I want you in my past
We moved way too fast and it showed and we did not last
A getaway
Maybe another country and I'll be okay
Out of sight out of mind type of thing I am no fling
Glad I didn't cling or get attached
A getaway
Far away
Out of your way
In my way
Just to say you're sorry I am in the way
Because nothing you can do could ever get me to stay

Latausha Bonner

One More Time

You say never again

While I'm sitting here like since when

I don't doubt you're done but just last week you ran to the first rung

I do not judge it's your situation

I just rather keep my distance before I give an opinion

What is right is right

But what is wrong is wrong

How come you cannot see what this man is doing is wrong and
that you two never belonged

Stop going along to his sad song

Singing you into misery

It's too much and too much history

You just rather be favored than to open your eyes and see

his behavior

You say never again while he continues to make friends

You say never again while he plays with your feelings and acts like
he cannot comprehend

One more time might end up being a long time filled with lies

Please open your eyes

The Other You

It does not matter if the feeling is different

Just as long as you give him some distance

Some men play dirty

Because you allow it thinking you're doing him a favor but deep

down inside you forgave her because little did he know you knew

That the other you may not know about you

She smiles in hopes there is no other you

But the five-minute calls and every other weekend staying home is

not enough for her to realize you three are in this too deep and

where did she go wrong

You investigating and going crazy trying to seem okay

When at any minute you can feel yourself about to crack

But no really attack because you know you gave 110 percent

Trying your best not to turn things into an argument because that

will draw him further down the road you and him are about to ride

on

In the back of your mind like we have a family "Come on"

But you know he is one that will never get it together

The worse feeling is knowing that you settled

And that the other you had a special part of you

And there is nothing more you can do

Latausha Bonner

But speak your mind, wait your turn, and hopefully, he will learn

And if not take turns or give him all to her and then maybe she will learn

Anticipating

Anticipating you

Anticipating everything I thought I knew

Anticipating that smile

But all I been hearing is your frown

Anticipating the love

But you told me plenty of times you could not put me above

Anticipating a call

But all day long heard nothing at all

Anticipation is killing me

Beginning to think you just want to be set free and get rid

of me

Anticipating

Should I have taken action

Just one real quick question

Thought the other way was not an option

So tell me what really happened

And you wonder why we have so much confusion

Never was my intention to hurt you

Anticipating

Use to think you were from heaven

Against a girl religion things I use to think about doing to you

So done

But still anticipating someone much like you

Sleep

I really kind of like this dude
But I think I'm trying too hard and not really in the mood
Want to get to know him more
But he's not putting forth effort at all so I'm not sure kind of
about to ignore
Depending on our surroundings and the company he keeps
he will not say a damn word to me
He is not trying to keep and I am very much to be kept
Booty call
Not at all
After the club
What you really take me of
I rather sleep
Than creep with you
I rather sleep
Then meet with you
Bored and very much tired of you
Sleep
Might as well
Our conversations, connection, and our sex is very
weak

What a waste
Mad we ever in life had to meet

Taste

I gave him a little taste
Now he blowing me up not giving me space
I have to face the fact I gave it up too fast
Now he getting on my nerves
These calls and text messages need to be put on blast
I should have thought it through
But was way too much in the mood
I danced on him
And gave him all I got
Bounced upon him
Never giving it another thought
I don't even like this dude
Just thought he was mad cool
It was late
I felt alone
Late night
Feeling right
He hit the right spot
Let's go all night
I put that ass to sleep
And wanted it on repeat

Latausha Bonner

But now I'm in my feelings
Thinking deeply, daydreaming, and dealing
Because I gave him a little taste
Now I have to walk around carrying mace

A Friend

What's the point in having a man when you can just have a friend

Talk the same, sex the same, or whatever you want to call it chill and Netflix the same

What's the point in being tied down

When I'm fine and all he wants is to be seen with me like he winning and they losing when he losing cause I can be out whenever I want

Still looking and don't know when I'm going to choose when

What's the point in having to be home at a certain time

When I like to get sexy and party

Talk to whoever I want with no apologies

And at the end of the night not answer my phone

Because I don't have to and have not had a man since four years June

When having a friend is just like having a man

Except I can choose when, see when, and forget when

A friend on my time a man on his time

Since you so smart tell me what's the point of having a man

A friend still going to love me

His ass still going to give me the best he got

He still going to spoil me

And he still going to sweep me off my feet

Latausha Bonner

Real shit though

Tell me what's the point of having a man

I don't want a headache

Because dudes are very insecure and they do not know how to love

I guess the lost love that didn't come from their mother can't come
when he grown

So now it's our fault they don't know how to love

It's easier dealing with a friend

One minute they are in love next minute they are running from us

Women have become much like men. They don't care to share or
be shared. They don't see their options. Women make excuses why
they don't want a man but actually hate the women that do have
men. We blame our past and the men we have been involved with
as being the reason we have become so cold. It's all a mental thing
and for this reason lots of women will remain single.

At The End Of The Day

At the end of the day, you put yourself with him

So don't play the victim like he only wanted to have sex just
you and him

These days you have to take the time to figure him out

All of that pointing of the finger like you innocent pointing him out

Believe me, I know where you're coming from

But you must admit the part you played in and stop running
from

Talking about he knew

No, girl, you must have known to

Because at the end of the day nothing slow about you

I'm just sure you let your guard down and revealed all to know
about you

Naive

Nervous

And too damn nice

Playing the victim does not mean he wrong and you right

Starting fights

Until daylight

And then disappear gone out of sight

What part did you play in this

Latausha Bonner

You going off at the mouth having too much to say about this
At the end of the day, it takes two
And now you're sitting there looking crazy wondering why he
ran from you

Space

Giving me space will leave room for another man to replace

Why not stay close

So we can keep that door closed

You think I'll stick around

With these late nights and fooling around

I have been around

And can see what this hitting for

I may sound insecure

Just don't know about you anymore

Space for what

Until you choose to do more or somewhat

Go on ahead and give me space

Because right now I am ready to replace

You may need me so just in case you want to keep me around

Choose who you want I am no girl to wait around

Our hearts are not here anymore so I'll just give you space so you can continue to fool around some more

Dudes know exactly why they cannot let a girl go. They will keep you close but just enough so you get attached and cannot let them go.

Ready Or Not

If men were smart they would see they can get more out of women
by doing their part

It's not a lot of work most men just do not think smart

Women are simple creatures

Men would know this if they looked deeper

Most men are nonchalant

And cannot help to not want more they just rather not

They fear more

They fear change

They fear commitment

And those type of guys are never consistent

Wanting more gives attitudes

Like your being disrespectful or rude

Wanting more causes arguments

Like what are you talking about say what you meant

Their confused and don't want to choose between his boys
and you

It's true most will put their boys before you

They don't want to choose between late night partying and you

It's true you will be their last option they will hardly choose you

These kinds of dudes will allow hate in their ear

Their just not strong enough and the fear of being judged is what
they fear
I will not ever disrespect a real man
They cannot do what they cannot see
Sweat, tears, and pain will not even make them change
It could be the times we live in but as a woman, I refuse to
take the blame
I don't care what age they are you cannot make someone
ready for you
And if you wait I'm a throw my hands up and pray to God
blessings are with you

Latausha Bonner

Less To Say

People change up so quick it's hard trusting someone

Good people have become scarce and even worse for good women

Men that know their stuff will even tell women to date around

So why you lost like "In a minute he will pick up or call"

People do what they feel

And if you're hurting he wasn't feeling it

Nothing will stop no one

So it might take two to know one

I'm not saying go out get your hopes up and become overwhelmed

But why not put your feelings first

This way it will be harder for you to get hurt

Deep down inside I know you love yourself

Red flags all over the place

He himself waves them in your face

But he feels your vulnerable, soft, and predictable

Dudes move according to how they can play you and get you to stay

Women are very smart needless to say

Scared

Scared to leave not because you love them but because they will be
with someone else better than you
Give me a minute
Scared to leave because you will be alone
Not stay because you actually love that person
Please give me a minute
Scared to love someone real in your life because of that fake
person who abused you still to this day using you
Please just give me a moment
Scared and nervous of the unknown
Go for it because soon it will show
Someone else could potentially be good for you
See self-doubt, not trusting self, low self-esteem, and being in your
comfort zone is the result of all this
Baby, I know you scared
But loving YOU is very rare

**Women are more scared to be alone than they are scared to be
happy!**

Add Pressure

You too easy going with whatever he wants to do

How about you do what you want to do making it hard on

you

Stop caring about who else he dealing with

Because I guarantee you if he messing with you she hard to deal

with

Men like it easy

But don't be too quick to please see

They also like a challenge

Been told here is where you need balance

Not too easy and not too hard to deal with

Friends or looking for something real

Sealed the deal

Or just looking for a feel

It all depends on what you two agreed upon

The easy way out is going to give no headaches

The easiest route is to please him

When in doubt ask no questions

But I'm here to give you some suggestions

Go hard for what you want

But never be easy

You will get what you want to believe me
Add pressure

Women who win add pressure

Seeking

Why feel bad about dating around
Them seeing it being negative is what I myself have found
Well how will you find the one for you if you never date around
Scared of their opinion so you stick around
Sad looking around at their happiness
While others laugh at this
I have no shame and refuse to live for you
Or what you say or how you move
I dance to the music of my life
Having fun and getting to know men is my right
Society puts so much pressure on women
Like their suppose to create this image be timid listen this was
written years ago
Life is way too short to sit and wait
You may never know what is your fate and who will come
along to love you and create a world with you
Never be scared of who will come along and judge you
Most of them are scared to be judged so don't let that stop you
Shop for men not just any man
Seek your soul mate
One you would have thought you couldn't ever relate

Cost

He thought he could buy my heart
But I still feel alone and very much far apart
The cost of happiness is at no additional price
So why do people walk around like "What if the price is
right"
Paying for love got you how far
Married people say they're so in love but feel so far apart
It could just be me and my beliefs
So why do you look so stuck in disbelief
My price way too high
Regardless of what you choose to go by
The amount of my happiness your bank account could not
hold
That checking and savings account overdrawn
You may need to rethink and pass upon
Because I know exactly what's going on
My price is way too high
And it actually cost nothing
But since you put a price tag on it be prepared to pay for this
loving
It cost to be the boss

Deserve

He will tell you that you deserve the world but won't give it to you

Tell you that you deserve better but won't do better with you

Smile in your face but behind your back do things to hurt you

Sex you so good in bed

Made a mistake and said go ahead

Girl he all in your head

Want more but got less

See messing with these type of dudes will have you thinking your life is a mess

When all you have to do is get rid of them so you can progress

I know it is a lot to process

But you under his spell

There is no way you can excel

I see so much potential

And think you should pay more attention to you

I see the real in you

You say you deserve better

All the while by him is where you settle

Lame

Shame some get overlooked because they are not popular
When the one she with is really not that into her
They say try someone new
When he the one you comfortable with and don't want

anyone new
She rather stay and not be appreciated
Then to go with him because he is not affiliated
Stay for the name and the games because that lame over

there the feelings couldn't ever be the same
I like to be seen as somebody
Instead of feel like somebody
He dresses nice, but him over there nothing looks right
I love the rush
When this lame right here might tell me to shut up hush
Lames are boring
Wild boys are balling
Is the little girl in her
The grown woman in her she keeps ignoring hoping she will score
She keeps going for those type of dudes and getting hurt
Same sex is more appealing now she does not want men

anymore

Latausha Bonner

Okay

Is it okay to love someone that does not love you

You can see their actions tell you

To keep daydreaming about something that will never happen

Sitting on the couch watching television like it will fall from the
sky

To pretend to be someone that you're not

Because it makes you feel better

To cry over someone that will never be yours

When you see them happy with someone else

To live a life that you yourself can see is not right

But pray on it later it will be alright

Well okay

Is it okay to say it's okay when it really is not okay to say

okay

Intimidated

I am tired of hearing women say men are intimidated by them

Real men know that being with strong women is when they will win

Men are not scared

They just rather stay away because they will not share

Strong minded women are what men seek out

They will not fall back without first seeing what you are all about

So what you make a lot of money

That will not draw men away honey

Independence is not why you're single

Your bored and just scared to mingle

There are some shy men out there

But girl please nothing will hold a man away from a woman he feels is rare

Your confidence is not holding them back

It's your attitude, no smile on your face that will make a man backtrack

Your pretty is not what's holding them back

Too many dudes approaching you will have a man take a step back

Latausha Bonner

You think you intimidate and use that as an excuse why you don't
date

You think you intimidate but want a man and can't wait

You think you intimidate but really not trying let's set the record
straight

You think you intimidate but you overdoing it let's not exaggerate

I am pretty sure a real man can handle you

Take advantage before a real woman makes an example out
of you

What They Think

I'm a say what they think

Because they scared of what you think so they don't ask thinking

just because you're a grown man you can read minds and going to

show out on their kids and their ride

I'm a say what they think because it's a thin line between what they

will do once they get sex and what they won't do waiting for sex

I'm not here for that grown man shit

True they are not all the same

Men's patience is not the same as women's

For this reason, they can move on, act like they don't know you,

and walk past you like "Please who are you"

I'm a say exactly what they think

Because instead of women telling them how they feel they fear the

unknown so they never ask instead they always wonder and that is

how you get your feelings hurt because men are different than

women

**You don't get paid to think, but you will pay a big
price by thinking you know what men think.**

Next

How many will you have to go through to get to know you

Everyone is not for you

Pick who you want but never put on a front

People are not fake they just in a rush to replace, have sex, and

on to the next

Again people are not fake everyone is just not for you

No one cares, no one loves you, and no one wants you to be just

for them

Have this thinking mentally

Put your feelings to the side then one day you will meet

you're all

How frustrating it is to give your all in hopes they will fall

in love

But they don't

Next

The same thing happens all over again

You give your all and put all your eggs in one basket and wonder

why you cannot win

I know I know I have sinned and been there over and over again

But you grow and you learn

You need no one to get to know you

The Core Truth of it all

On to the next, just make sure it's you who they won't ever neglect
but instead will have mad respect

Latausha Bonner

Grow

Seems to me like this thing is moving kind of slow

Don't mean to sound like I want to fall right in love but I

just want to know

A call and a visit here and there

Is this suppose to be fair

When you already told me at the door you don't share

I know we didn't put that title on it that you're my man

So how long will we remain, friends

Maybe move one level up and become best friends

Soon to be lovers and friends

But no for real will you be my man

I just want to know can we grow and if we can't will you

eventually, let me know

Somebody In Anybody

Can't be trying to look for somebody in anybody

Chasing somebody in anybody

Trying to love somebody in anybody

Crying over anybody searching for that somebody

Stressing over anybody because you want that somebody

Losing sleep over anybody stressing may never find that somebody

Falling in love with anybody scared may never find that real love with that somebody

Holding on to anybody may never let go

What is the use where is my somebody

Together but alone with anybody

Because you have no patience to sit, pray, and wait on that somebody

So you go for anything in that anybody

LOVE IS BLIND

Temporary Souls

You got your feelings hurt because you cared
Put your feelings to the side
Fine people got ugly souls to
You cared to share what hurt you
What use to break you
Weak men will listen and ask deeper questions to hurt you
They never really cared
They just don't care and want you to stick around
pretending that what you shared made them care about you
So what about you
But really temporary and it never was about you
In and out
Polluting the air
Never missed a teardrop so I can see why you thought he
cared
Temporary people do love hard at the beginning
But soon reality shows and they will have your head spinning
You never really missed a thing you were just hoping and wishing
But that is where you went wrong temporary souls barely listen
So how could you ever have that vision
Here to steal your soul and have you depressed

Feeling less and very stressed

So I tell you no lie

Pay attention to temporary

Everyone's heart is not pure it's immature

They will still want more

But it's up to you to make sure you do not fall for the same

temporary souls anymore

Old News

What is old is someone else new
What is used is someone else brand new
Since you think you cannot move on because of time
Please explain to me how time has failed you
You wished for the best
While he was wishing for someone else
You remained faithful
While he continued to show he was ungrateful
He constantly says you will find no one better
You don't believe in you and agrees there is no one better
You rather die than be alone
Your dependent on him and cannot hold your own
You have shown him you have his back no matter what
Believe it or not, he been watching and always have known
He smelt the weakness in you
He saw that you were nice
He heard that you would be with whatever
It's nothing new just another you
Your old news
You're off your focus
Put the old up for a very low price

Your something new is what a new dude cannot wait to try
and he will not even question or think twice or ask why

The Help

Continue to be the help

Answering your phone because they are going through

problems needing advice and for you to solve them

They are really not that interested in you

What is more interesting is your ear to hear, your availability to

chill, how fast you pick up the phone, and an answer once

they knock on your door

Your life is their life

What do you guys mostly talk about on the phone

Tired still on the phone till the crack of dawn

The help is so selfless while the other so selfish

But hey they like you and so into you

Not

You are the help

Actually temporary help until they feel you have done enough and

helped

You helped them get through their problems with their baby dad or
baby mom

You helped them get through hate, their financial situation, and

their dark times

But they like you and are so into you

Not

You are the help and they will replace you because you have satisfied their needs

They will look you in your eyes with a straight face and tell you that they need you

But in reality, they just need someone to talk to

Know how you are wanted and where things are going by the things you guys talk about. You cannot possibly be that nice. It's levels to everything. Nothing more always less. You could forever be help for them and for someone else

Latausha Bonner

Kept Secret

Who would have known

We got a thing of our own

Even though you have a family of your own

Said you had feelings long ago

Told you a few words ago I have control

We get into it and you say "Watch your tone"

Wish I had one of you to own

Wish I had a clone

Many nights went alone

Scared of the dark and of the unknown

Let alone you leaving me and not telling me so

But we have grown and know I have to stay in my zone

Now staring at my cellular phone waiting for a text or a call to
ignore

But sure I'll probably answer or text right back to get ignored

Best kept secret

Or just your weakness

Distraction

Men are not a distraction
Just ask them
It's all about what you desire
So don't come around me like his ass fine and conversations
are fire
Something is wrong if you cannot focus during your day
He is the only thing on your mind if you didn't notice an attitude
throughout your day
What you feel is what you think in turn it's what you speak
Never satisfied and cannot wait until night to get dressed
because she knows all the spots to greet and meet
Nothing is wrong if you have your life together
There are just too many females that cannot wait to meet a man
like it's now or never
The distraction is your not focused
So there is no way you should be approaching
The distraction is your bored
Him coming into your life seems like your only reward
The distraction is the thought that you are not enough
So maybe that is why you come across like your so tough
All I am saying is do not call men distractions

They too laid back and cool just ask them

Women will let a man that does not like them distract them from work, their goals, and their children. Men will let themselves be a distraction if women let them. I say those men are not going anywhere. Take care of you first they will be there when you are mentally ready.

Hater

We kissed

Girl that does not mean he loves you

We made love

Still, it does not mean he loves you

He took me to meet his boys

Girl that still does not mean he loves you

He planted a seed in me

What that proves

It does not mean he loves you

He sex me so good

Girl he just playing that role

It still does not mean he loves you

He took me shopping

Call me a hater but it still does not mean he loves you

Let me explain

Call me a hater but dudes will play that role very well

Their bored or tired of what they had so they looking for
something
new

Your that something new

Maybe he does love you

And girl maybe he does care

But please don't put all your eggs in one basket

Dudes are here one minute and gone the next

You cannot possibly think shopping, sex, or meeting people means

anything

Dudes do that with females they do not even know

Some money to waste on you

A baby that may have been a mistake

Please

No hater just being real

Lie to yourself all you want

I had to learn the hard way and I am pretty sure you will too

Tempted

We all get tempted

Alone rejected because you attempted to do what was best

for you

You didn't invest enough for you

Never took enough time for you

So you released your power because you thought there was

still some fire

Lighted the match no fire

No desire

No fireworks

Just thought you could see what would work

Denial got you stuck

Never thought you would ever go back

Can't tell you anything but good luck

You failed got scared and tempted

Never missed a beat

You thought you two connected

But a nobody in disguise

Your heart lied to you and none of this should come as a surprise
to you

You fell in love with their physical

Latausha Bonner

And chose not to question their mental
The visible things about a person we choose to love but the
invisible things about a person are what we should be in search of
You were not tempted
Just admit you missed it

Him

I always wonder who he is
What he is doing
Is he married already
Or searching for me in every her he meets
Scared to look because I might find him and not him
While I am laying here thinking is he at work or in a strip
club
Um...do he even has kids
Or waiting for me to make that move
I may open up to see what happens
Just hoping I do not open up to the wrong him
He could be all I need
Even though we never agreed
Or nothing I need
Misleading me
Anyway
Tell him I am going to find him because he could
potentially be all for me or nothing indeed

Latausha Bonner

Entertainment

People know how to get to you
Don't always accept materialistic things in front of you
They will use what they gave you to get to you
Sad but true
Stop always entertaining what's hot and new
Because soon you will have to choose between him and
what was never used
I'm not saying entertain the old
But entertaining the new could confuse you
The grass is not always greener on the other side
That dude you had couldn't wait to ride or die
Now you're new want new instead of you
New is sometimes entertainment
No strings attached and are only looking for relations

Carefully Listen

I do not want to be his number one

I want to be his only one

I do not want to be his favorite

Because in my mind another chick is made for him

I do not want to be cool or his friend

Because in my mind he will never really have anything to

show me

Pay attention to words or you will get your feelings hurt thinking

it's one way when it is another

Words hurt but actions show

Latausha Bonner

Love You Hate You

I must be crazy if I love you

But I can't fake it

Trying to erase it

Can't shake it

Can't help it

Got to do something about it

Even though I love it

Something about you I can't get over

At one time I hated you

Tried to love you

Never put any one above you

Always was there for you

Trying to heal all the pain

Trying to gain any lose of love I had

Mad even sad I met you

Inside and out I still love you

Trying to find a place with you

But whichever way it goes

I still love and hate you

Another Day

Another day think about me but for right now forget me

Don't think about all my mistakes I did yesterday or the day before because she was not me

Another day love me because right now I have an attitude

Another day say you care to want to be with me

Another day share your dreams, hopes, and wishes with me

Another day choose me because today I know she wants you

Another day care about my feelings but for right now say you could care less

Another day it will be you but right now I am feeling someone else

Another day chase me but for right now replace me

Another day live for me but for right now die for me

Another day let's grow together but for right now whatever has been planted is dead

Another day smile with me but for right now a frown is what you will see

Another day you can do all these things

Just not today

Many people do not know their worth. Instead of putting their foot down because they know what they deserve they will go for anything as long as their mate does not leave their life.

Settle

Women we settle because we want that feeling

Let's be real we all want someone ready and willing

I don't know one single woman out there that do not want a man

And if she says she does not I will never understand

We all say don't settle

All the while being the main ones settling

Can't blame them because most are battling with themselves

Most don't love themselves

So they go out and look for themselves

That extra person

Extra love

Extra happiness

Or even an extra feeling to belong

A lot of people are brought up wrong

And they really don't know

Looking for anyone to agree and show some love

Even if that love is not a guarantee

"It's okay at least someone believes in me"

"He sees me"

"He belongs to me"

Blind but not really blind because you can see

Me being the person I grew up to be was never unsure
Opened my eyes and I refuse to ignore or be ignored
Be secure in you
That way you will never get played or ever get close to settle

Latausha Bonner

My Cry

I cry for peace

I cry for sleep

I cry for help

Come save me

You know I'm lonely

You know I'm afraid

You know I'm shy

You see me hide

With no one by my side

I cry for them to hear me

Save me

But they ignore

Whoever you are please hear my cry

Never ignore someone that is telling you they need help, but they may not be telling you with words. Your love will make a change in their life. A change you never would have known. God is using you for them.

Maybe

Maybe I'm confused but I don't want to lose

Maybe I need help but I can't find anyone else

Maybe I'm wrong for keeping you up this long

Maybe I need to let loose and have a little fun but I don't

want to mess up

Maybe I need to rest but I don't want to miss out on what is

going on

Maybe I need to find some work but I'm so tired

Maybe I need you

Maybe I need you

Maybe it's your fault why I feel this way

But maybe I am confused

And maybe I do need help

Maybe I don't need you

Get rid of you then maybe all these confused feelings will go away

Never blame someone for the way you feel unless they are the
actual cause for the way you feel. Meditate and pray will help you
figure out why you feel the way you feel. Other people are not to
blame. Maybe it is just you!

Latausha Bonner

Mixed Emotions

Should I love you and try

Or hold back feels like I'm going to die

Should we break up and say our whole relationship was

made up and a lie

Or stay together and tie the knot that's been untied

My love is like a roller coaster

One minute it's so strong then the next I have to help it along

Yeah we do have our ups and downs but let's make our ups strong
for when we do have our downs

Emotions run high in my mind and I can't seem to put them in
words

But be patient with me so I can figure out how to make things
work

From the time we met till now yeah things have changed but let's

talk to rearrange those changed things

Throughout the years truthfulness was lost

And then I came across this none caring attitude like

"You're no different"

Yeah these emotions that are running high through me I'm trying to

get low so we can move this thing here right along

Why do you feel
Confused and Used
And who is to blame

Latausha Bonner

Love Is Like

Love is a sign telling you him or her

It's like your life just started when you found love or ended

When you found love you could be the happiest person on earth or
soon to feel sadness

It could be like your floating to heaven or sinking to hell

Love could make you want to bring life to this earth or end one

Love is like a curse

It could make someone steal or give

Love is so confusing

But one cannot pretend, hide, or ignore

When it's in your face you feel it like a knife and it's sore

Take advantage or try to ignore

Want more for sure or even try to ignore

I am trying to tell you it will hit hard and with that, I am pretty sure

Just Enough Is Not Enough part 2

Remember when I told you Mariah wanted her body touched

Well lately I've been in a rush to get my body touched

Just enough was just enough when I first met you

Getting to know your name your personality and what you wanted
for your future

Just enough was just enough that first night

Just enough was just enough that first couple of months

But now with just enough, I'm a little confused

With just enough, I am not happy

You give me just enough

A kiss and a hug

Am I not attractive

I mean what is it for real

So I guess just enough is just enough with some people

But just not enough for me

You can be selfish when wanting more. If a person is not pleasing
you how you want then make that decision and move on. It's your
life you have to live with certain things, and if those things are not
making you happy do not hesitate or you will live with much
regret.

Latausha Bonner

How About You And I

See I know you feel for me and no doubt I feel for you

And it is true that at the beginning things went smooth and
you're a very cool laid back kind of dude

So why do I feel like a fool or have been fooled

The connection is there and I feel we can be together for a long
time

But as we sit here you and I know that you're not mine

All kinds of fine, sweet, and kind

Just me and you we talk about everything

Sitting here I wish you could be my everything

I know it's something not even close to nothing

Kind of wish I knew

But I don't have a damn clue

Maybe in a few more months, it could be you and an I

But your situation is much different from mine

See I'm free and can do me

While you're on the low

I say why not just go with the flow

And you never know

Yeah I can go on with this forever

It never hurt to say how you feel

Trying to keep it real

Feeling the way I feel

While I want more but too unsure because I am not for sure

So how about you and I just try a little harder and take this thing a

little farther

Spreading Yourself Thin

Spreading yourself way too thin

Too many men in your face it's hard for you to think

Close your eyes point your finger and choose

Make it quick because a good man is one you will lose

Date after date

Shit gets old when you're in a rush

I have no more respect they no longer want it early they want you
late

Tired

My mistakes and picking the wrong men

Might as well walk in his shoes so we can relate

Chill in his feelings

Feel his soul

Read his mind

And be comfortable in his home

Seeing through him, looking straight at me, through me

Any way to get to me

Because vibes are not on our side and if not him then who

Men love spreading themselves thin, but us women are happy even

feel blessed when we finally meet one real guy

we like and can relate to

Empty Emotions

For us to be sitting here and not saying a word
Talking about other people and what we heard
No doubt feelings are there
But scared of what the other will say
Not to quick to make a move
Thinking it's going to mess with his grove
Kills me the most because I like him so much
But him not too much in a rush to make me his woman kind
of sucks
We should let our bodies do the talking
This night is not going the way I thought it
We fighting our true emotions
A lesson learned just know this I should have thought this through
before I wrote this
No chemistry
Trying to figure out what made you fall for me
But still just me just him sitting so close to each other but feeling
so far apart

Night Walker

He always makes sure he sees me

And throughout the day he makes sure he shows me he
needs me

Go through a little something during the day

But slides through and I give him a little something during the
night

Even though I know it's not right

There is something inside me telling me not to put up a
fight

Got a thing for him that is more than a like

Stay up all night talking about our likes and dislikes

Got a night walker dressed in all black

Many times I want to give him all back

Because pain and revenge is what I see in the near future

Don't only judge me it takes two

But in the end, I know I will be the only one to lose

I need a morning walker and an evening walker to go along with
my night walker

So the question is not who he is, but how long will I let him stay

and only remain my night walker

So Wrong Too Right

What am I doing so wrong

Or am I doing so right he can't believe it so he runs or be

some time with me to see how I'm going to react

What am I doing so wrong

Or am I doing just right and too right is not what he want

He wants a headache the arguing and fighting

Might be attractive to him

What am I doing so wrong

Or am I doing perfectly right that he scared

Scared of another commitment and running from one

relationship to the next which is totally understandable

What am I doing so wrong

Or could it be I'm doing too much right that it overwhelms him and
got him thinking too right is going to

eventually get too wrong

Well, I came to a conclusion Miss. Too Right can't possibly be

with Mr. Too Wrong

Most time women will question why a man will not commit. Just
remember it is not you if you know in your heart you did nothing
wrong. It is him, so let him go. And if he does come back around
you will know how to handle him for sure.

Questioning Your Motives

I'm so perplexed

Mine and your situation has become a mess

You got me confused, dumbfounded, and kind of worried at the
same damn time

I thought you and I would be a little more by this time

Didn't know your and my intentions were not the same

Boy you got my mind going insane

Happy you a real man though

Happy you let me know how you felt about me though

You let it go and so it flowed

Mentioned on a daily basis you have a lot of responsibilities

You have been to my crib does that not tell you I got the

capability

Your girl got many abilities

You got me questioning my womanhood

Got me taking a second look at my motherhood

You got me all types of very misunderstood

A little confused though

Some things you have to clarify so I can let go

Our connection

Boy you show so much affection

Our conversation

Boy you let me in on a lot of information

Point being

I'm a human being who caught feelings

Does the real man in you not find that very much appealing

But

My inner thoughts are begging you
Even though I want to strangle you
Can admit that I love you
And that is just what I hate about you
A couple days
Well let me help you out a couple never
Because I don't know who you think you are
You took what I said way too far
But But
You said you loved me
Why didn't you repeat it after me
An argument
I swear I told you everything I meant
Wish I never met you
Wish I hated you and could hate on you
But you got that
And for your sake hope you never want me back

Just Fine

When the love of your life walks out your life

And in the back of your mind, you say your just fine

What really does that mean when once upon a time you were all mine

Truthfully on a scale from one to nine, I thought you and I were a nine

Came to find out you just a five

Our hope not alive

Feel like a doctor

Should I revive

We did survive so many years of this

But these past couple months a girl felt too deprived

All and all I'm just fine

Still trying to find out what that means

I saw this from afar

Took you a while to make me feel like a queen

Felt like I was in between her and her

But I never intervene

Still trying to figure out why you walking out my life I'm just fine

Guess I have to use this as a sign

Love never lived here

Latausha Bonner

And with that, I'm just fine

True

Power

Chapter Three

Hate to Love

Time To Go

When he starts getting all in your face
When he call you out your name
Lord only knows what's gonna happen
When he put his hands on you
When he starts talking mess
You know what to do
Give him the boot time to go
Maybe you had to go through it
Him trying to talk to another female
Trying to be a player
You know what to do
Take the key kick him out change the locks give him the
boot it's time to go
What about the time he told you he didn't like what you
were wearing
So he told you to take it off

If you didn't buy it don't tell me what to put on

You know what to do

Pack his bags throw them out the window give him the boot you got to go

What about the time you found phone numbers in his

pockets

Lord only knows what is gonna happen

He better get down on his hands and knees and prays to the good God above

Kick him out give him the boot time to go

If you are going through all the above and more

Take the key kick him out change the locks give him the

boot

Baby, it's time to go

I Just Love Your Lies

I just love your lies because you tell them over and over again

I just love your lies because I will still sleep with you at the end of the day

I just love your lies because I still feed you

I love your lies because I still smile

I must be in love with your lies because I know I am not the only woman

I am in love with your lies because I know the truth but I stay hoping you change but your ass still remain the same

Most times women will stay not because they love what the man is doing, but because they hope he will change. Understand no one can be changed, they have to want to change, but only for the person, they see a future with. If he stays the same regardless of how faithful you been to him you must understand the hard truth he cannot see you in his future and he does not care about your feelings. When someone truly loves you he will work on himself for you.

See, this all is okay, find yourself, find your happiness, and move right along with your head up high.

WIPE YOUR TEARS

It's time to go out and find your man

Physical Me

Kiss a would have

Sex my brain

Have oral sex with my thoughts

Because the way we moving might not ever lay next to each

other and play out the sex plays that we thought

Chill with my inner me

Massage the bitter part out of me

Talk nasty to the scared part of me

Because the way we going about things you may not ever see the

physical me

Finger the part when I said "Forget you"

And while your down there don't forget to taste it

Because the way I feel no other part of me is willing to love we

I rather I be emotionally unstable than me ever be too sexual

Physically in bed with you

Staring at you when I know damn well no part of me could

ever be with you

I'm a mighty good ass woman

Guess you thought the might in us was too tight to ever lose touch

Phone calls got you confident

Nightcaps got you to the point nothing could ever possibly go

wrong with us
Hate to burst your bubble but the mental, physical, emotional, even
the sexual part has never been strong enough within us
Tried to make up with me but myself wasn't going for it and
I just chilling around for the sake of us but know damn well too
much has gone down for feelings of lust to come back around for
much more then a second round
Won't be looking back at this laughing
Can't even crack a smile at this when asked when
Cause the shame on a man's face when he knows he lost
spelled out "Try again"
But some men are not humble so they rather lose than win
Keep undressing me with your eyes and sexing me with your
thoughts
Cause the physical me you will never connect to physically

A Set Up

It's a conspiracy

You walking around like "Hey do you remember me"

When he really doesn't

He attended to her every need

Won't be seen with you cause that's another problem their
relationship really don't need

Don't fall for that

He plotting against you

And from the beginning he had his mind made up

Drake said it was something to do when he had nothing to

do

So what you think he doing, girl he a dude to

He might call you

Sit outside your house to make sure you being loyal

Say words to you in public like he's feeling you like that

When he really got one female on his mind and girl it's not you

It's all apart of his plan

Steve Harvey tried telling you all men have a plan

And the plan is to set you up into thinking he eventually wants

only you when in reality girl he just looking for something extra
and new to do

Hurt Men

Too many hurt men
They cry, complain, turn around, and sin the same way
It's their excuse for not loving women the right way
Instead of addressing their hurt they push real women out
the way
Instead of confronting the person that hurt them they push
everyone away
But they claim their men
A hurt man is the worst
I don't care how strong, confident, or for sure you are in
yourself
If you stay with a hurt man long enough they will break you
down and have you questioning yourself
They play the blame game
And are to never blame for the same shit they caused
At this point, it's easy to blame yourself
Take a moment pause I doubt the amount of stress he is giving you
when added up is all yours
He is fragile and whatever he is dealing with is too hard to battle
He has manipulated you
And you have forgotten about you

Hurt men do the most

Because it's never their fault even when done the worst

They will look you dead in your eyes tears rolling down

their face asking for a second chance

And you being the woman you are saying "Okay but this

can never happen again"

Hurt men come from all races

Just be aware because it's very easy to blame self and miss it

Had Enough

You look rough

Guess you had enough

When enough is enough people become victims

When victims get nervous they lie

When a liar gets caught he can no longer hide

When found he lies to cover up lies

When the lie no longer satisfies the blame game magnifies

When called out no one is by his side

His weak mentality can no longer fake

When fake people get scared they run till the heat in the
kitchen cools down

He will come back around for love still

A good woman will forgive

He does not want to talk about it

In hopes, you will forget about it

All the while standing outside throwing rocks at this glass house

His home

The one he took for granted but thinks he still belongs

No exaggeration

I know you don't want to be on your own

No passes

I'll come on hard and strong

You're right he wrong but choose not to care because in his mind your his and can't be alone

You showed him enough

He did way too much

Now you're done and had enough

Latausha Bonner

But I Never Loved Them

Some hide me

While others are proud and could not wait to reveal me

Some kept me on a hush

While others were never in a rush

Some only seen sex

While others weren't even pressed

Some had me on a team

While others knew I wasn't anything like the rest

Some mentioned I'm weak

While others said you a bad chick

Some said I'm worth it

While others leaned back like "Shit who is she"

Most spoiled

While others said she don't deserve it

I never cared who did what, said what, or thought what

I never loved one

So best believe he still out there training his mind for just one

Someone like me

I have been very honest with myself when it comes to men. Most females won't because they really cannot see that they are the problem

Ashamed To

Chivalry is dead

They're not opening doors when walking in and out of restaurants

They're not opening car doors when being picked up or dropped off

Walking ahead of the female instead of behind like "Baby watch your step, take my hand, and please take your time"

Social media got them feeling themselves like without it their not "The man", taking pictures like these females, too much time on their hands and laying up in bed figuring out what next to post

It's whatever but instead of being better they blame women like we don't have enough on our plate, like we don't have kids running around, trying to figure out different ways to make time

Like the hurtful things that come from the same men's mouth that's suppose to care don't hurt

The truth is right there dead in your face but pride got you feeling ashamed so you make up any false statements trying to erase the beauty in a woman

Breaking her down is easier than building her up

Saying "I see you, keep doing what you doing", is too much

Your dry mouth and chapped lips all in denial

Because each and every woman is not to blame for the hurt your

mama gave

For not seeing yourself as the beautiful man you are inside

Your insecurities rubbing women the wrong way

You being scared to be loved pushing someone away in love with you

But who do we blame

Ourselves

And I know you have feelings too but that is no excuse for the way you speak about women so openly

This one thing you should be ashamed of

But it's become so normal

I salute the real men who are ashamed to

Growing Young

Men are not getting older
Mentally they are getting younger
Could be the types of women they pick
Or it is just them not caring is really what just makes me sick
Men are not getting older
It's their actions that show
They talk like little boys, act like little boys, then get mad at
women like me for coming for them
Thinking they are sending for me
When they should be arrested for hurting feelings
You feel me
They do not measure up
Saying us women just can't keep up
They don't stick around
Saying it's our attitudes why they don't wait around
We are nothing like their mother's
But blame us for not playing house and catering to them like they
are our sons
Weak
Breakable at any moment
Soft

And can't say anything to them without them blowing up
Never should have had anything to do with us women
But who am I but a mad woman
I've got wisher
While the men around me growing younger

White On Rice

So laid up gone have me paid up

I guarantee you what I'm about to speak is not made up

Hope you prayed up cause you swear the shit you do is cool

I got a thing for you but choose to never be a fool

Putting all women in the same category like we used goods

I rather sleep alone than to be with you and feel lonely

I rather eat alone than to prepare meals for you like we one

You see

Swear no one above you

Well we gone see

Cause no man ever made me feel broke to the point I didn't

let him see

I'm all over what you been doing like white on rice

And despite the truth, I took you back like we were brand new

Like no one knew

Like I was made for you

And the generosity in me kept wanting to give you me

But the lost part of me still couldn't agree

But the power that never left me kept embodying me

So I had no choice but for you to set me up and help me

leave

Latausha Bonner

Down Low

Everybody has somebody on the low

Too busy complaining to love the one you with have to have
someone on the side

Shit be mad real but I guess everyone applies

The lies they tell never hides

No shame you can see it in their eyes

And it will come to no surprise that your man himself to applies

I tell no lies or no tall tales

Look at me crazy but your the one who fails

"It's his fault, not mine", but girl you hit it on the nail

Subject yourself to pain no wonder you look out of it

He revealed him and everything changed

Everyone on the low

That's why I refuse to be the good caring girl cause they swear you

slow

Control This

I got this
Never been the one to be dissed
He got me feeling like I'm getting ready to dismiss
Then soon I'll be the one he missed
Cause I know he under much stress
Told him plenty of times I'm better than the rest
But I also understand he got to do what's best
Yes in his favor but mine much less
Have to have control
But the more I think about it I want him much more
Control
Don't have to worry about me calling out of control
Or see him in public and getting out of control
Or dissing him and balling out of control
I can admit me and him been creeping out of control
You could say we going ham and out of control
But as a whole and all alone we good
Body and soul good God I swear this man stole
I got the control I got this
But what's better for me is not you so I have to dismiss

Confessions

I want to fuck

But no luck

I want my bills paid

But not trying to get laid

I want a man

But not a demanding man

I want money

So no one can run me

When will it be my turn

Tired of people telling me to wait your turn sit back and learn

Everybody so fake

Wonder why I take breaks

Cause you won't break my heart

Try to make me your wife

And then tear me apart

Fake love

Fake hugs

Fakes rubs

I rather be alone before I mess with any of you scrubs

Absolutely Not

Hoping you can come

Relax it was nothing but a touch

Stuck

Really don't care

Has to suck

Overthinking

Over analyzing

Over nothing

Messing with me will get your feelings all excited over nothing

There is nothing like rejection

Especially when you think you like someone

But no really want to wife someone

In hopes, you could sex that one

But in reality, you confused

Never knew what to do with a chick so amused

Can't talk straight and at this point your confused

When you absolutely thought she was the one but the grin on her
face said absolutely not

You thought you had a winner and could win her

Sorry you thought you had a winner

When absolutes and the yes man in you and the confidence

you held could have never steered you so wrong putting your life
on hold for this long

I kid you not

Those thoughts had you in your feelings I know

With a real woman, you can grow

But cheating you will reap what you sow

Pretend

I can walk past you like I never knew you

Once upon a time, you was something I was hoping to do

Dreaming to screw

Straight wishing for you

Your dress code had a girl on hold

Froze in place

Phone calls were never enough

We have been doing a lot of pretending though

Your fallback game weak just wanted to let you know

I peep the showing up fresh fade Gucci wear just to put on a show

I have no respect for you so do not come my way talking fast and walking slow

I'll circle around you smelling fresh and new

But I'll look away pretending I don't know you

Looking past you since you want attention and hoping I'll be the one to pursue

Boy just look at you

I won't fall for you I'll hop over you and run from you

Your pretending and I guarantee you will miss it

I'm over it so it does not look like you're going to be him

Intuition

Love is not all we need

What kind of fairy tale ass story are you living in

Keep them compliments

The type of woman I am is obvious

You don't have enough sense to try harder

But see I have a backup plan thinking smarter

Call me whatever you want

I already knew what it was

It's too late to come back to a never was

The intuition in me was kicking in

So now that you ready no chilling and sitting still

Five steps ahead of you

Almost thought you could get the best of me

Spread yourself way too thin

Now you looking stupid like let me in

I might have been the stupid one

But I'll be damned to just let you in

My heart wants to let you in

But the intuition in me won't let you break in

Women possess something that you men just don't have

While you guys are saying it's all in our heads

It's nothing that can be described
Some women don't show they deny
But for the rest of us, we will never hide nor deny
Not giving a damn about you or your pride
Smart women will listen to their intuition
They will send you on your way hoping and wishing

Imagine

Why do I feel like I'm the one to submit

Got me walking around with a smile on my face thinking

you the one who will commit

So dumb and super submissive I have been

Looking me in my face thanking me for how supportive I been

Imagine that

Just knew I would be that

But you're not all that not even close

So I don't have a clue why you thought you would be

favored over most

I got too much dignity

Thought you could put the fear in me

I feel myself way too much to care if you leave or stay

So please pack your bags today

I have no patience for you to delay

I imagine a peace of mind

I know I can get right

Being able to sleep all night

No headaches to wake up to a clear eyesight

Pretending I don't know what to do with you

At this point, I'm imagining something different and he is just

not you

Regret

He will regret losing me

You just don't know any better but he knows and once he

calls you will pick up the phone

Guys know who they dealing with

That is why they pick to fall back, relax, then come back

What you got the next chick do to

So why would you think you're the one and he's the one that does
not have a clue

Men know exactly the type of women they have

Rather he hides you or wife you is all up to you

Yes it's you who has the power

Men do not have enough manpower but they are given all

the power

Men do not have any superpowers over women

So how it is that they constantly winning

Most of them will not regret because they know the game

They cheat and create their own rules

Some love playing women and make them feel like fools

Most do not know the golden rule because hey majority rules

He too cool, too smooth, and will not have a problem replacing
you

It's not he will regret

You just keep letting him and you will continue to be played and upset

Clock

Time stops for no one
You said I'm fake but it takes one to know one
Time heals all
But see this dude was never around and there for me when I
fall
In time we will know
But the clock shows the time
There is no way to fast forward or rewind
I never had time
But you sure made time to lie
Steady running out of time to talk
The time or the clock cannot save you this time
I am too fine to wait around for your time
Got too much confidence to stick around full-time
I have never been a part-time
I have no extra downtime to play with you in this lifetime
Stop thinking I am too available
In the meantime, I'll get with you
Just had to run that back to you one good time

Problem

You're the problem

Stop walking around like "He needs to grow up" solve him

He too grown to change

No man is ever the same around different women

What you give is what you get

So get this

Relax always be you with no regret

I have no problem with women trying

It becomes a problem when you crying lying saying he trying

Because God knows you lying

While he in the background smiling

Knowing he got you right where he wants you

He stunts putting on mad fronts

You deserve more

But can't see that in fear you will never get more

I am here to reassure you that you can do better

I understand you want to make sure

See he's immature and cannot ever have more to do with you

You too damn mature

Get him out your view so you can see who been hiding in

your rear view

Latausha Bonner

The problem is you too forgiving
Now it's time for you to start reliving

Jewelry

We all like gifts

In the back of our minds creating a list

Some dudes will make it hard for you because they were not raised
to give and uplift

They were raised to take to sit and wait

They are not givers or a man who delivers

They have mad excuses

You will never be his or even be exclusive

A man looking to keep knows what it takes

So do not bother with their excuses men were born to hunt

and take

They will dine, buy, and surprise

So do not ever listen to them if they don't even try

Money is not the issue

He just does not see you in his future

You're in his right now

Men love to see a woman smile

So never say he is trying when you are always crying

You're in denial

But special and is entitled

Men are hunters by nature

Latausha Bonner

Some cannot wait to find a female to chase her
To love her
To spoil her
To cherish her
Picnics, candlelight dinners, jewelry, or some flowers are simple
You being in a relationship or being single should not hold him
back so what you guys are not official
Men know who and what they deserve just like women
Never believe him when he says he does not deserve you
because you told him what you expect
He did not expect you to come that direct and it affected his
view of you
He did not know what to say back or be a man like he is
supposed to
Men will spend
Depending on the female is the only issue in the end

Consistency

Consistency does not mean you winning

It's too blind me because nothing has changed since you been in

Same old routine

Yeah I know I'm mean

But I mean I'm bored

And the way my life going I cannot afford to look towards just anything

Empty promises

To go along with all you promised me

Not solid

You typical common and I bought in

I will never understand what I actually saw in you

My only option

But just for the time being

Got busy now I lost him

See consistency means nothing if the true them is not that into you

Some dudes are only consistent so no other man can have you!

Latausha Bonner

Off

I get turned off so easily

Can't find someone wanting to please me

All they do is tease me

Ease me

Always displeasing me

Just a little

No man is ready for it

Hungry for it

Craving for it

Lazy

No one ever amazed me

A little bit

Being to hesitant

Scared

Or showing me in plain sight they really just don't care

I am not confused

Just want to feel used

Especially if I like dude

Riding, talking, loving on him

Something is off

Never turned on

Never ready
Or is it just me

Latausha Bonner

That Is Just How It Be

You clean, cook, and wash his clothes but he lies
You loyal, truthful, and obey but he makes you cry
Your loving, respectful, and his yes girl but he still will not buy
you the world girl
I am trying to tell you that is just how it be
Why can't you just let him go so you can feel set free
What are you holding on to girl
A headache, a stomachache, and a heartache
Make me want to shake you
You cannot see how fake he is to you
For God sake
You're a blessing
But you continuously stressing, depressing, possessing
But for what
That is his way to shut you up
But I am saying that is just how it be
And with time I hope you listen and agree with me

There is no excuse for how some people treat others, but some
people are just set in their ways. If you know they will not change
let them go because you know how they are in real life.

Sex

No woman ever had the power to make a man stay
So stuck on come get it get around each other and have
nothing else to say
It's early but wishing he would stay
The crying just nothing else to say
It's all the same
Your not superwoman
It all lays out the same
Blow him up
Put it down
Laid up
Shut shit down
But in the end, he still leaves
We have been here before you should have believed me
You gave your all
And in the end, it all still falls
You lost
Yea you lost it all
I have no sympathy
Cause, after all, I told you your ass still wasn't feeling me
Here and glad to sin but done and gone with the wind

Latausha Bonner

You knew it wasn't him
So why did you think by only using sex you were able to
keep him and trick him to stay

The Juice

Drip drop

I got the juice

They mad because we were introduced

I can't entertain the excused

I got a lot on my mind

I can't chill I refuse

Ready and feel a little loose

Not scared will never hold back I refuse

Glad to be living

Staying positive is what I choose

A bright future and feel so amused

They can't touch me and have no clue

Pretend what I'm preaching is fresh and new

I can admit I slipped up a few times

But my past does not define my new it's mine

My juice bittersweet

Cross the line and you're out the door to creep and cheat

Keep taking my nice for weakness this juice will pour from you to a new dude

Latausha Bonner

In The Way

Why do certain dudes even approach certain women

He already knows he does not have his shit together to do so

I will never understand interrupting her life

You have nothing going on in hopes of a might

Leave her where she at

You so blinded by her body you attack

Sex appeal is real

But dang you want nothing further let's keep it real

What you have to offer

Standing their eye contact won't stop her

Want her just to say you had her

Now what's the logic in that

All just to bag her

Single and hard working

A conversation so you can see that person

Mind games so you can see what's working

Move fast so she won't ask any questions about your past

Text all day because in your real world folks won't agree and have

things to say

Say she something special so she blinded by who next to her

Waste her time so real men have no time

Make her cry then make up to show you done and want to make up

You just in the way

Nothing you can defend or say

In the way of real men that will actually be there for her and gladly lead the way

It is true no good men will be in the way on purpose because they know for a fact real good men are watching you!

Only Concern

My only concern is us

Why you so concerned why they concerned about us

Why our love is just not enough

Seems fake and rushed

I remember when you use to love and lust

Guess that gets old

It's never enough

Repeat just don't feel the same

Rewind please no seconds for me

Pause I couldn't live like this forever

Stop it's the end let's just admit

My concern is us

While your concern is them hating on us

I thought I was the female in this

You being the dude shouldn't be consumed by females all up in the

mix

I should be your only concern

Guess that's a lesson learned

The outside world should not be your concern

My definition of a man was all wrong

Or it is just you being too concerned about it all

Time

The right thing for me is not on your time
Feeling like I have to break my life story down like a
timeline
I wouldn't be going through this if you weren't so damn fine
Even when I dig deeper into your looks and character is a thin line
Boy we on MY TIME
Tired of pushing me in the back all the time
Is your situation bigger and more important than mine
Boy stop lying
You think I won't have to make sacrifices
You never once sacrificed this
Like I got time and you don't
One thing you won't do is drive me crazy
Crazy mentally
Because I'm feeling you sexually
But see that cannot be the excuse
Because you choose to do you while I waste my time taking
the option to lose
Liking someone and even loving you is not worth me
wasting my time
Boy I never was blind

Just too damn kind, and again I will never let you waste another
second of my rhymes

Fall Back

I don't get attached

I just relax

It wasn't that good anyway

So I have to take a step back

Fallback

Hurry back

You were a one hit

So no need to reminisce

You fine and all

But everything else just not at all

I don't ask for much

But every now and then just the right touch

But you got too much going on

And every now and then you act too tough

But you're a dude it's in you to hit and forget

But you messed with the right one

I'll hit and forget and have you running back like "How you forget"

Loser

Take advantage so you won't lose her
Because too many walking around that will choose her
If you are not worried I think you should
That next guy will do everything you wish you would
If you the truth then have no worries
I guess it's because you have mad shorties
One woman is worth a thousand bitches
And I guarantee you that one can satisfy all your wishes
Hey who am I
I think I talk too much
I am not tripping
Why would you assume such
Loser
Take for granted abuse her
Use her
And misuse her
Not one real woman will stick by you
Keep going for those ones who will trick by you
The loser in you cannot see the winner in her
So go ahead move to the side so he can see the winner within her

It's Dead

When love is not there
And everyone involved no longer cares
Fear has got the best of you
And hate has got the rest in you
No communication
No information
Just don't know how long I can tolerate this
Just lay up and ignore
Crazy because I use to be the only one you adored
Now it's time to hit the door backdoor because obviously, I
am not the one you're looking for any more
Let's just dead the situation
Because I can tell you have other reservations
Too much energy
Boy you done took the very last in me
It's been a long time since you last touched me
And even longer since the last, you loved me
Dead it and please do not forget I said it

Latausha Bonner

Butterfly

Your bomb

I will not understand how you sitting there so calm

Take no mess

Give up

Give him back to the rest

You have evolved

Your soul cannot take him anymore

No way you should have been involved

You have been through many different stages

Many different changes

And dark places

Your beautiful and highly favored

You need to tell that dude bye to see you later

Your appearance, your shape, your tone, and your attitude

will draw them to you

From what I see no flaws at all

Grow your wings and don't be scared to meet guys that will make
you feel alive

At this stage in your life and from here on out do everything right
by you

Your crown did not fall but it's tipping catch it before it falls

We all go through those times in life believe me
But now your glowing and girl it's showing

Done

No, you can't be for real
Thought we just sealed the deal
Fake, uncaring, and too unreal
It's crazy because I see the real or is it just the way your lips feel
But dealing with you we calling this real
Did not take much time to reveal
Cause I'm late didn't catch the memo
Must have missed that train on to the next demo
Because things never last but things could be so simple
However, you had your mind made up
And chose to sleep with whomever
But whatever
Whichever way I decide to go I hope it's far away from you
Cause to tell you the truth I think you been knew
Knew who and what you wanted to do
Heard you had a crew
Word around town you have a few
See I know what that is hitting for
And with you, I cannot ignore
My heart is in pieces
And my attitude is ready for revenge

Should I avenge or change my ways
Boy I tell you all men are all the same
Listen here you cannot be done
Because she meaning me left a very long time ago

Wasted

Wasted Tears
So many wasted years
Wasted time
You wasted so much of my time
Wasted happiness
Need to find another way to get around this
Wasted energy
Wish you only seen the inner me
Wasted love
When I continuously put you above
Wasted sleep
Wish I was the one you choose to keep
A waste of you
A waste of me
Wasted cries
Boy now without you I have so much time

Signs

They always give signs
In between a hi and a bye
They always give signs
Like you stupid, you will not understand why
I am trying to tell you they always give signs
Better open up your eyes and find out why
Boy oh boy they always give signs
And look at you sitting there wondering why
I tried telling you they always give signs
And no matter what you will never matter
In the end, they always give signs
He told you he was going through a bunch of BS
Read between the lines and see it was with his ex

Some dudes are not over the person they were last with. Most dudes are not over their child's mother. Be careful who you date. If he talks too much about her he still wants her. He is not around you to spend time with you and talks about her. He is around you and talks about her because he misses her and needs someone to talk to. Do not be no shoulder for a man to cry on when it comes to another woman that he loves. But of course it depends on what you want from him and if you really like him or just want to be his friend.

Latausha Bonner

Type Dudes

Type dudes that want a meal every time you turn around
Want some head every time you turn around
Type dudes that do not have rent every month
They have to be the center of attention type dudes
I have kids but I do not have kids type dudes
Baby why you tripping type dudes
Let me borrow your car type dudes
I got you when I have it type dudes
The ones you have to watch around other females type dudes
Them one dollar dudes
Cannot take a girl out to eat type dudes
Baby, you deserve better type dudes
Pack your bags run to your mama house type dudes
Phone stay close but when I call don't answer type dudes
How much is the cable bill type dudes
Want to argue and leave when rent due type dudes
Scared to confront another dude type dudes
Baby when you get off work type dudes
Call you right back type dudes
Better not be talking to no other dudes type dudes
I am the best you ever had type dudes

When you enter they exit type dudes

Let me borrow something type dudes

Should I continue...

Type dudes about to be really mad about this right here type dudes

Rotten

I am no good to any dude

I have bigger things on my mind

It's okay call me rude

Single, kids, and a dream too big to fall asleep

Tired

Busy

It has become easy to miss me

On the run

No games or playing just for fun

I have to set an example

Sometimes it is too much to handle

On the phone with you for what

You know how much information I can learn

I can taste success and I'm yearning for the best

Lay up with you for what

That is not paying

Sorry I am just saying

Big dreams will cause a change

So you mean to tell me all about life is a job a check after paying
bills nothing but some change

I have to make a change

Be the change

Live in my change

At times I do get uncomfortable

But my passion and drive fills the unknown and makes it
comfortable

I am telling you this cannot be life

Life will not stop, pause, give you time to think, and no strikes

But life as I call it today and what I see in my future is nothing
alike

I don't have excuses

Just figuring out a different way to do this

It has become easy for me to be forgotten

I am not rotten

I just know there is more to life than just this so it is okay for a
minute to be forgotten

Latausha Bonner

Second To None

Do not make me your last

Make me your first

The way your moving I am going to be apart of your past

I rather be passed last than be first

Apart of no team which means I am first

Second to none and damn for sure going to win

This generation so messed up

You first you second

You last you first depending on how they feel

I am just keeping it real

I rather deal, chill, settle it's whatever

Depending on the weather

Get it together I will not ever settle

I need certainty

Many guarantees

My life is not based on how you feel for that day

I will not move according to how you feel

What is the deal

Second to none and I promise you I am going to win

Miss Me

He always talking about miss me with the BS

Soon he is going to be the one to miss me with his BS

He has not seen my best yet

He will regret be upset cause he neglect

Miss me

No, miss me

Miss the availability I gave him

Miss all the love inside me he already knew

Miss my yes

Since I known him never been a no

Miss the pop-ups

Because for now on every door will be locked up

Miss me

No, miss me

Over And Under

I once heard the saying "The best way to get over someone is to
get under someone else"

Well why is it so hard to get over

Make me feel some type of way because he has not come

around for me to get over

So I'm dealing with him trying my best to get over

Have to stay busy to get over

Can't be alone to get over

Ignore to get over

Keep looking to get under

Deal with whoever to get under

Lie to myself to get over

Or stay stuck and stay under

Over this boy

Over the lies

Over him making me think I'm the one tripping

Over him making me think I'm the one going crazy

Over being played as a dummy

Over the secrets just recently revealed

Time to get up under a real man

Up under an honest man

Up under a real thing

Up under a truthful man

Want to get up under someone who tells the truth when it hurt

I cannot wait to get over this and up under that

Time Flies And People Change

I always thought we would grow up and do this thing together
Guess I'm a little delusional shit don't last forever
But listen
The conversations I had with you I never had with anyone though
But time flies and people change
Never thought I would have to rearrange or even change
and it's so strange
We in two different lanes
Once rode on the same lane
Same thoughts
Same dreams
Silent treatments when we once couldn't shut each other up
We were a bad ass team you and I
But sadly we let the little things disrupt or ups, our dreams,
and you and I
Time flies and people change
Just know my love for you will always remain the same

I Hate To Love You

All I want is to be done

But every time I talk to you I end up listening,

I sit, and can't run

All I want is to ignore every word coming out your mouth

But every time you come around I end up taking that same
stressful ass route

All I want is to disappear from you

But once I do I catch heart since you the one I always knew

All I should have done was not say hi

Cause now I'm in between a bye and a cry

I hate this love shit

Wish I could have been a one hit

Because nothing is coming out of this love shit

Nothing has changed

May need to rearrange how true I've been with myself

Cause a girl doesn't have the energy to hate and be in love

with you all at the same damn time

Married Men

Married men
Scared to marry a man
These married men act more single than these single men
All up in a single woman's face
Can't wait for the night
Things happen that can't be erased
Feelings coming from a selfish place
Scared of who's watching
Carefully moving
Not letting an interesting text or phone call in the way of
how he secretly moving
No strings attached no feelings no emotions
In and out your life is what he's hoping
Scared to hurt feelings but not caring about your feelings
who he's hurting
Call it dumb but we all are humans who want to feel the
need to belong and be loved
And rather he has a home and kids waiting at home is
what's not thought of
The fact that he's a married man who shows attention and
touches the right places is a thought all its own

Crazy Love

This love is a headache
One minute I'm in love
The next minute I really don't care
This love got me feeling like giving up
But I know true love won't let me
This love and my love got me running
Running to no destination
Running because I don't want any more of the fake love
making
Got me missing buses and calling off work
Dang even waking up like this is too much work
Wish we would get it together and show some teamwork
This love makes me want to scream
Because you never believed in me
Our love is a mess
And this is way too much stress for one person to lay to rest

Since Hello You Had To Go part 3

It could have been perfect

He left out my door and never said a word or let me know

This could have been my fault

But he had problems of his own

He had to resolve his own shit

And took me on a roller coaster ride

And denied it all to my face even tried to hide

Told you before I been fooled

This man wasn't so perfect after all

Wasted my time couldn't wait for me to fall

I always thought the older the better

But that is not true just depends on the type of man you

want for you

Since hello you had to go

Because since the beginning you were not invested in it

Things Just Happen

Stop crying

What you crying for

It is over and done with

Crying will not change the situation

Lying did not help your situation

Cops won't stop the situation

Damn you for sure cannot resolve the situation

So slow down

Take a breath

Just a damn minute where is your man

Why he leave you to take the blame

Such a shame

But out of my range

Why you screaming at me

Thought I could be a friend

Now I'm all types of B's and to hell with me

Don't believe me when I'm telling the truth

Let me go

But just know that things just happen

Get over it and you will soon realize your man was not ever

just your man

Latausha Bonner

And he had another secret lover in the end

Treat Me No Good

Have you ever met someone you liked a lot and no matter how bad
they treat you do not care

Why

Because you were blind in love

But not literally blind you just thought you loved them

Listen

Treat me how you want to

Show me no respect

And every time I look at you don't hesitate to get upset

Treat me how you want to

Curse me out all the time

And never mind my feelings

Cause it's your time to shine

Show me no love

Put money above me

Get yours

Put me down

Cheat on me

Steal my money and leave me for broke

Lie to me and don't apologize for doing so

When I don't want to give it

Take it

And when I don't like it

Make me hate it

But please please don't make me cry

Because I have too much damn pride

So many people live in this fantasy world of how they want a person to treat them. You are the only person that can get real with you. Realize what a person is doing to you. Face it and then replace it

Thief

I once heard you cannot be happy with someone that already has

someone

Someone that already has someone is like a thief putting your life
on hold

While they enjoying theirs with that someone else

Stealing your years

Stealing your love

Stealing your happiness

Sitting around waiting

But waiting for what

For him to leave after how many years

I then had to tell myself "Girl you a damn fool you

don't even believe that"

So what you going to do...

Wait... Then reality hit

I have to make a choice

And the bad part about that is it has to be made alone

This dude stealing my companionship

My agreement with someone

Stole my choices made with someone

My eye-to-eye with someone

Latausha Bonner

Not a thief in the night

But a thief in daylight

Made a fool of myself

Now I feel I have nothing to give another because he took it all from me

Do not let anyone steal your years and have you put on hold because they have someone else and want you to sit back and watch. Live your single life alone or live your life with someone who is not in a relationship. I have to admit I had to learn the hard way and no I'm not here to judge anyone. Just know there are more single people in the world than married or in a relationship. I promise you will find someone for you.

And also realize if the other person is okay with you waiting around they really don't care about you because that is beyond selfish.

Holidays Hurt

Sideline chicks play themselves
Come Valentine's, Mother's, or Christmas day find
themselves by themselves
Sideline chicks play themselves
Want to get mad at him because he with her and you by yourself
Opening gifts by yourself
Candlelight dinners by yourself
Damn holidays hurt for sideline chicks
Monica said they were sideline hoes
But I like to call them sideline chicks looking for love in all wrong
places
Looking for some of that love he gave her
Just want to be loved
But really don't want to hurt anyone
Why do holidays hurt for sideline chicks
Saying he playing you when you really playing yourself
Cause girl you knew
You knew he was in love
You knew he had a family
You knew you were not going to wake up to him in the morning
You knew you two wouldn't lay there long

But girl I can relate
I do know that holidays hurt for sideline chicks

Choosing

Everyone choosing

Everyone losing

People walking around sad and with the blues in

Choosing someone nowadays got me choosing

But every man walking up to me I stay refusing

I should take advantage

But instead I abuse him to confuse

him misuse him just might reuse him

Because I'm running out of options

Years ago I just know I lost him

Latausha Bonner

Tiptoe

This dude tried to tiptoe into my heart

He almost had me but my heart kept falling apart

He couldn't handle my past

It kept slapping him in the face so I knew this dude

wouldn't last

I came with too many opinions

He never had a good comeback and thought I was trying to run
him

My strong mind revealed all of his weaknesses

So I knew I had to end me and him

My looks blinded him

Couldn't help but to remind him of what he had

I had no sympathy

And I could not relate not an ounce of empathy

He tiptoed, stumbled, and threw his hands up like "What's up"

Fist up, stood up, and I had to push him back into reality

Because this dude really thought he had me

Too many scars

That got us nowhere so far

Too much pain

To the point, we cannot live together sane

You tiptoed
But I been let go

Latausha Bonner

Dark

Becomes

Light

Chapter Four

The Real

Your Life

You need a variety of people in your life
Especially when you have certain people in your life who don't
care about what is going on in your life
Nowadays you need a backup friend, backup family, and a backup
man
Putting people in your life may feel like an exam
Why dealing with people feel like you been scammed
Like Goddamn
Damn any kind of relationship then
Every person I meet putting them on the witness stand
When will I get a break
Loyal friends so hard to make
People walking around on some real shit like snakes
All they want is to take take take
Too many times I have to take a double take
This shit right here man gives me a stomachache

Latausha Bonner

Dealing with this on and off on a daily basis

Puts a toll on your body I swear people need to get their lives together

I'm not Miss. Perfect

But it's hard for me not to observe it

Phone Calls

We live in a generation where people don't talk on the phone
So how in the hell do they keep their relationships strong
Even got Facebook and Instagram full of people talking
about "What's up y'all"
Wyd and good morning text are the norms
No wonder people don't last that shit is played out and boring
No one has any conversation but wants so much
Let me say that again...
No one has any conversation but expects so much
And they wonder why they get ignored
Hell I'm bored
Big bored
Little bored
O Lord
So you can't afford a decent conversation
And for the record, I'm not up on all these
abbreviations
Hell
I just learned wyd and ttyl
How do you do it
Hearing a voice would be nice

Latausha Bonner

A little laughter in your voice would be nice
But hey it's your choice
No conversation and when we do it sounds rehearsed
Give me a morning call
An I love you call
I need to talk to you so I called call
I just missed your call
What you up to get up call
I heard I didn't text I called call
It's a shame stuff got this bad
A text over a simple phone call has things really got that
bad

Hell

How do you look like you been through hell
Scared and ready to sell
Sell meaning to join because it's the easy way out
"Your so pretty I never would have known"
"You don't look like you been through that for real"
"Who would have known"
How do you look like you been through hell
Scared and at any point ready to sell
If I looked like what I been through it wouldn't be a pretty sight
If I looked like what I been through you would say "She's been through hell"
Boy if I looked like what I been through you wouldn't be as friendly
I'm glad I keep what is in so it does not come out
The past where it is at so it cannot run about
My true feelings in so they cannot find what is in
A smile on my face so they cannot tell I'm ready to break
Confidence instead of the hell with all of this
Some positive in my life so you cannot see the negativity
Hell how do you look like you been through hell
Unprepared, impaired, scared, and at any point in time ready to sell

I C U

This is dedicated to all single mothers who take care of her
children and do not ask for help or any handouts
I love you guys

I see you sweating
Baby, I see you stressing
Baby daddy don't care
But dammit take care of the kids, anyway
No time for her
Her time for them
Them them
Them four or five kids
Them who needs clothes
Them who need to eat
Them who don't care to understand that mommy tired
Them who can't seem to comprehend that mommy hungry
Them who cant understand that mommy unhappy
But she puts herself last
School, two jobs, no car, no money, and bills
Bills
When will they end

Strong, courageous, fabulous, love, patient, and wonderful
Women, I love your strength
Keep it up because God is watching and Karma is to

Latausha Bonner

Intent

Nowadays you have to spell stuff out to people
Like hi bye it was nice to meet you
I'm not all into you getting to know me
What are your intentions
We have no connections
Sorry you had to waste any of your expressions
People too sneaky to me
In and out of everyone's business repeating it back to me
So if you doing that to them I would be dumb to think you not
doing it to me
What you intended is for shit not to hit the floor
But what do you expect as the middleman each side always
want more
The middleman always catch heat first
Cause neither party wants to admit their wrongs or that they did the
worst
"I'm just a messenger" Is what you will hear on the regular
You say your intentions were good
When I see the intent was to spread hate

Be careful who you surround yourself with. People are filled with hate. Their way of getting it out is to make sure people who may know you or not hear bad things about you.

YOU ARE STRONGER THAN YOUR HATERS

Influenced

Stay away from people that know you're doing wrong but
influence it

They love to see someone doing worse than them so they influence
it

Rather they see the good in you or not they influence it

With their silence they influence

With their yes they influence

With their agreeing they influence

With their smile they influence

With their arms wide open they influence

People will support you and act like it's not you

People will support you and push you to fail

Look you dead in your face and try to sell you your fail

It is true they will support you and push you over the cliff

And do not turn your back because they will lie and say look who

pushed you over the cliff

It is not their fault especially if you seem happy

Supporting your failures most are glad to be

Some will support for the better of you

Others will support the bitter they have of you

Know the difference there is a lot done out of bitterness

To The Limit

Push me to the limit

Push me to the edge

And if I get nervous don't be afraid to tell me to stop being a punk

jump over the ledge

Test my intelligence

Grade my performance

And anytime I complain tell me, in the end, it will be all worth it

Please sign me up to fail

Because I already know I'm going to win

Say my mentality so weak

But see my mind so strong

I don't blame you because I am going to outperform

You're lazy

But so amazing

Unable

But incredibly able

A joke

But I'm not playing I'm not going broke

Push me to the limit

I am a strong woman I knew when we started you would never listen

Let what people say negative about you and their negative thinking about you motivate you. Stop reacting to them, stop hurting, and stop giving it attention. Don't you know or have any clue what people go through in their personal life? If they even see you smiling they have a problem with that. Don't mind them!

Money Talks

Why should money be the only reason why people take action
You know money buys things not life
Money will turn best friends into worse enemies
Money can separate the closest of family members
Because of money people die
Because of money people suffer
Lack of money got people starving
Money got you thinking "I'm going to be big and blow up"
Money got you forgetting family
The thought of money got you forgetting to love
Money got you killing your neighbor, your sister, your brother, and even your mother
It's the thought of money that got people forgetting the most important things in life and that is LIFE

New

Drake said "No new friends"

But I say, new friends, if the ones you around bring you down

Break you down

Talk bad about you and have you feeling lowdown, sad, and off track

Friends will hold you back

Even will try to get you to pick up there slack

Family will do it to

Sometimes the best thing for you to do is fallback, check

back, or sometimes attack to gain back your respect just to get back on track

Relationships are hard

Never settle if it's a friend, a family member, or something

you are trying to gain much greater

Not intentionally

But people will hold you back and bring negativity into your life

Not because you both are going through something but because they are going through something

Look out, a toxic relationship is one of the worse ones to have

And those are not friends just ones pretending to be down just to stick around

Come For You

When you on your shit people will come for you
Because they know blessings are upon you
They know everywhere you go you shine
They hate they sitting in the dark in the background
It bothers them when you smile
So even when you bothered still smile
They do not like how attracted people are to you
So never change the fact that people are drawn to you
You damned if you do damned if you don't
So do not ever live life trying to please everyone because
believe me, they won't respect it they just won't
Your name will make their temperature go up
Like you physically did something to them so they ready to run up
The way you walk will bother them
I'm telling you they will feel you sending for them
They can never stop your moves or your blessings owed to you
I say let them come
Because you're about to explode right in front of them

Latausha Bonner

Rest

I do not like being negative
Decided to take a rest at this
Wish the devil might run up
Trying to figure out a way to come up
He thinks he got me mentally
Well I'll get at him physically
Because he has broke mankind all the way down
Got to run, flip, skip somehow
Got to ignore, sing, pray somehow
Still, have to find ways
Love ways to smile laugh somehow
Emotionally a wreck
Next step is to rest

Motivation

Whatever you feel you were created for should be your motivation

It's your creation

And should motivate you

Encourage you

Elevate you

Inspire you

And drive you

Whatever you feel you were created for should be your motivation

Since there are no limitations to what you yourself can do it should excite you

Ignite you

Renew you

And move you

We were not born for anything

We all are born to do something

What really is your purpose

Who are you as a person

Find out and be determined

Learn it

Pursue it

Get excited

Latausha Bonner

Tell the world about it
And do not ever hide it

Get Excited About Something

Down Fall

Keep letting people be your downfall

They don't care about you not one bit at all

They see you weak and need someone just to say you have
someone

They're using you as their backup when they mad at their main one

Get your priorities straight

How can you compare what you need and ways to stay

straight with them

Forget them

I promise you will not regret them

How can you still be stuck in the same position with them

Hoping things will go on forever with them

Even though I know we are all on our own time and

different situations with them

But let's be clear stop acting like we don't know

Because I knew as soon as you introduced them to me

I felt it was something negative that you should know

I am not the brightest

And I promise you I am not biased

But I know for a fact that person will be your downfall

But I understand right now y'all only having a ball

Latausha Bonner

Just please answer when I call because nothing positive is
coming out of this at all

Ready

It is not right when people want you to date when they are ready to see you with someone

Want you to chill when they ready

Want you to be happy when they ready

Want you to love when they ready

Want you to be alone when they ready

Want you to be depressed when they ready

People will want your life to be based on how their life currently is

If their happy you happy

If they break up you have to be broken up

Or they will give you bad news to make you want to be broken up

When they broke the thought of you having money gives them an attitude

Any less or anymore they will not be happy for you

But who's life is it really

People will unintentionally want your life to be just like theirs. For this reason, I say to get around like minded people because if you are trying to better your life that should not have anything to do with them but it does.

I know you want smiles on other people's face. I know you want love, I know you want hugs, I know you want them to be proud of you, I know you want to be respected, but this cannot always be the case depending on the people you place yourself around.

DO YOU WHEN YOU READY

Night Life

Okay during the day
Work hard to play hard at night
The drinking and drugs cannot fight the feelings
So she has till two A.M. to ignore those feelings
Dressed up, a fake smile, and dance so they cannot tell
Gives whoever want it knowing she going to hell
Deep and all upon it ready to sell
Attitude on ten and ready to snap
Because confidence is what she herself lacks
Everyone is fake except for her and her crew
Get out the way because before they enter you already knew
Standing by the bar hoping she will be offered a drink
Because after the club he is the one is what she think
Just can't wait
That nightlife every night always feel right
Then music off, lights on, drinks down
The worse feeling for a female who loves getting down
Two A.M. means home alone
"Can't wait for tomorrow it's too dark too quiet and I'm all
alone"
Flashbacks of her nightlife come on strong

Never knew what she was doing could ever have affected her and
be considered wrong

Energy

Feel people out
Get to know what they are all about
No negative energy during the process
Just learn your win and you're loses
You only have the energy for you
Two is way too many so choose who you give your energy to
People will take away from you
I don't have a lot of energy
Too many people fake and not a friend to me
Not too many get a lot of chances
I do not put myself in a lot of circumstances
So no second chances
You give them a little and they take a lot
You fought and brought more to the table
People will take advantage
I'm wondering what you thought
I cannot take how selfish people really are
But then again I forgot too many were raised and untaught
In a world full of people I rather be alone
Or is it the people I have been around that's in the wrong
No extra energy

People are really heartless
You have to really learn who is for you regardless of so
much selfishness
I have no extra energy
So please keep that from around me

Clap

Everyone is not going to clap
You took them out of their comfort zone and they cannot
wrap their heads around your success
Yes it's true your success will have other people stressed
Your comfort becomes their discomfort
Your love becomes their hate
Your beginning is their end
People swear they own your life and you have to tell them
all about your sleepless days and nights
It is not because they care but it's because they know you
are rare and see it as not being fair that you made it out
Out the storm
Out your situation
Out of your struggle
Everyone cannot handle your hustle
You have been through enough bad times and struggles
You owe no one nothing just remain humble
Don't just take my word for it
Announce it and see their mouths drop
I always knew you could do it and never stop
Look at their faces

The kisses

The hugs

After you announce it see if any ounce in them actually changes

They cannot clap because they are not on your level

Please do not try to level with them

Explain to them

Feel guilty

Or try to relate to them

Your goals and dreams make you different

Do you see why they see you as a threat and different

You don't need their clap, their hugs, their congratulations, or

their love

Remain confident and rely on you

Clap your own way all the way to the top

You will find a new family and also loving friends

But in the meantime never stop

Tell Me Something Real

I don't want to hear about how much money you made today
No, it is not hate I just don't like being around the fake
It's all good and gravy you went to the mall and got a new pair of
shoes
But let's be real you really cannot afford them
Don't call me up telling me how drunk or high you got last night
And that fight you almost got into with so-and-so
Cause I might hang up on you because you are not in the
right
Got pregnant by a married man
She says he's going to become her husband
Now let's be real
He's not leaving his wife despite the way you feel
You in too deep
Give it up
I had enough
Like them moms that say they love their kids but put a
man before them
Or like the kids, out there getting treated differently because of
their skin color, race, or hair texture
Or people that get married and bring kids into this world

Latausha Bonner

because they thought it would be fun
I don't want to hear about nonsense just the real
You can leave them fake stories for someone else to hear

Truth And Guilt

Truth always has a smile on her face

And Truth never cries

She likes to make people feel bad

Truth also likes to break up families and best friends

Truth can lie though and have people thinking she is telling the truth

Truth also wears many faces and have everyone confused

Truth never walks she runs

Runs in and out of people's lives

Truth can be involved in one person's life throughout the day

Truth will even agree to get married till death do them part

That person might try to forget Truth but Truth has her way of making one remember and hurting them all over again

The only way a person can get rid of Truth is, to tell the truth

Then Truth will run to the next person

Truth's best friend is Guilt

Truth and Guilt run together

Not Yours

Have you ever wanted something you can't have

And the more and more you think about it you get mad

See I think people should be more happy with what they have

But many of them looking around at what everyone else has

Soon they will find themselves unhappy and stressed

When they should be looking at what's best and feel much blessed

But I guess they choose to press for much more

So sure the success feel so secure

But nevertheless

He wants that car

She wants that ring

They want that house

May feel like you settling

But what really is unsettling is what you have is staring you

right in your face and those are NOT YOURS

Too many people like to look around at what everyone else have and got going on. **WORRY ABOUT YOURSELF** and stay in your financial lane. Get secure with yourself.

Snap Back

When you snap back they tell you to chill out to go have a seat relax

When you speak up they tell you to shut up before you lose

When you stand out they crowd around you because they know you're the one they will choose

When you do you they tell you that you're wrong change because in reality there is no way you could ever be that strong

When you don't give up they start to hate hoping you will get discouraged and eventually will give up

When you have a good heart they start to pick with you but remember your smart no hater could ever leave such a mark on you

Snap back

Snap back but not in the same way they do

Never let what someone do to you change you

You are highly favored and this is for a reason

Stay calm you know in your heart it's your season

You are on a mission

Do it because you love it not just for a commission

Don't fall short, fallback, or look back

Snap back, glow up, even show up

You got it

And don't let anyone ever try and take it

Moist

You have a choice
Most choose the comfortable choice
I choose the uncomfortable choice
Stay low because they think they have no other approach
Unhappy so you mean to tell me that was your approach
You own your world
So why live in a dream world
It's all reality
Please whatever you do take me seriously
You say it's yours but you constantly doubt
But what about
No what about your dreams
If you can dream it you can live it
So why waste time sit and think about it
You were once all right about it
But got sidetracked and scared
But once upon a time you really had to care
Keep those dreams alive, moist, and real
They may appear unreal
But by never giving up you never know what you could
ever reveal

Dark

Anything you do good will come back to you

Out here doing dirt like it won't get back to you

Rematch with you

Calling back to you

Or start reaching out to you

Dark spaces kept secrets

Growing up there is nothing beneath me

Hurt places are dark places

It is really hard to get out of those places

The world is against you

Seems like everything you do you lose

You pray

No change

You change

But everything around you stays the same

You read

You sing

You praise

But nothing

You don't seem too lucky

We all have been there so don't stare or judge

Give a helping hand in hopes they will budge

Get Involved

Life is what you make it
Sometimes you can't ask you just have to take it
Make the best of it
Then the rest will fall into place
It's a lot of competition
So don't get sidetracked in fear you will miss it
Miss out
Thinking you getting out
No way around this life
Do right and right will be done by you
I get it I promise you I do
But giving up can get the best of you
But I promise you if you back down now they will replace you
I'm sure you're close
Pulling back now you may never know your full potential at
it's most
Go all the way or don't even start
I believe in you why give up now before you even start
Get involved
And never back down

Knowledge

Knowledge is power

It's not about having fun it's about being aware

It's not about not caring it's about educating yourself to care

It's not about following it's about standing out so people
will want to follow you

Not one person knows everything

But it sure takes a strong person to stand up and speak about what
they believe in

What I don't know you will have the information on

So don't ever doubt the mind and what it is educated on

Stand strong and firm in what you believe in

But first, gain the knowledge so you can properly repeat it

Do not ever hesitate to stand up for what's right

People are not wrong they just choose not to fight

No education and confused

So that is why they need you

Anything anyone ever knew or did came from someone else

It's like a chain reaction

Just waiting for something to happen

People may be clueless because they do not know where to
start

Latausha Bonner

Strong minds do think alike
So start a movement and fight with all your might

Hide My Shine

I do tend to hide behind my hair
Because everywhere I go they tend to stare
I don't know if they love or hate
But with most of them, I couldn't ever relate
I'm shy but cool and loud at the same time
One day I will find someone willing and ready to ride
I don't know what's come over me
I feel silly, ready. and goofy all at the same time feeling me
But don't let that fool you
Choose whatever you choose to do
I play no games
No play station PS nothing tablet type of lame
I come around when I come around
Why you taking my moves so damn personal
I have stuff I have to do
And you too damn rude so I'll pass
Move with your stank attitude
Call me what you want but I don't hate to get hated on
I hide and get hated on
Not around and get hated on
Love and get hated on

Latausha Bonner

Chill and still get hated on

It's all good

But one thing I cannot control nor hide is my shine and that is the

real issue you have

It's okay just do not get out of line

Try to jump the line

Talk too loud in line

Or say you're tired of standing in line

Because that line is way too long of fools that cannot reach me

P.S. Keep watching me

Softy

Females too hard and dudes too soft

Wonder why the respect has been lost

Never knew there would come a time I feel more like a man than the man

They ought to be ashamed

Lames blame everything on a woman

Dry, mad, baby mama, child support, court hiring, warrant having,

stressing his mama doesn't have anything for his asking ass lame

Nowhere to stay

So he has to get with such-and-such just to have somewhere to lay

Let us pray

Please bow your heads

Lord, please let us pray

Cause never in my thirty years have I seen this coming

Put his butt on blast

Men in the past would never go for this

Such a disgrace to the human race

No example

Praying these streets gone bless him

But they stress him

Imprison him

Latausha Bonner

And kill him
Straight softy
Dear Lord, please let us pray for them
Softy
Sorry you lost me

You Are Money

Who you are is money
What you are made of is money
What you know is money
Your voice is money
Your talk game is money
How you approach things is money
Your appearance is money
What you want in life is money
How you go about things is money
Who you surround yourself with is money
What you learn is money
Your presence is money
Your future is money
Baby, everything about you is money

Latausha Bonner

Better

All my life I been told I think I'm better than somebody

But that is just confidence I AM SOMEBODY

Maybe you need to get your life right and you will feel like somebody

Somebody special

Somebody amazing

Somebody important

Maybe you mad at that somebody you let play you and

bring you down

Maybe that somebody has confidence issues and you let

that rub off on you

Maybe that somebody does not love themselves and you let

them play you and rub off on you

But you know what I think

I think that somebody really is you

You have control over you

Me being somebody should not stop you from becoming

somebody to

Never Say Never

It was a time in her life when she was proud of herself

But then a day came that she would have to test herself

She didn't see it coming

It hit her in the face

Once she knew it happened

She tried to change her ways

At first, no one knew of it

Not even herself

But when she did know it she swore it would go with her to her grave

She could not see how it happened to her

Misleading her day to day

Now

Never got her every way

You are not special or exempt from anything

Never say never

Latausha Bonner

Never Give Up

Grab him by the balls

Ride the shit out of him

Make him come not once but twice they love that

And when he comes come with him

Exaggerate the mess out of it

Yes

Yes baby

Lick him on the neck

Rub his back

Make him sweat

When he begs you to stop

Tell him you have to get all you can out of him

Make them believe you are the best

Because it's too many people standing in line

I don't care about anything he talking about

Go get yours

Break him down

Make them cry

And when he says he is down to his last replace him

We can't deal with the broke

Time is money

And no I am not acting funny

I have no mercy for anyone or anything trying to hold me back from my dream

Use them

And if they have nothing else to give

Have nothing more to say

Make it the best he has ever had

Mess his head all up

This world will take you and treat you like gold then spit you back out. If you do not take control it will ruin you and it will not care I am telling you.

So y'all thought I was talking about having sex. No, but still put your all into whatever you want out of life

P.S. NEVER GIVE UP ON YOUR DREAM

Latausha Bonner

Not New To This

I don't care if you knew me

Just accept the new me

Cause I don't live back there no more

You look confused, dumbfounded, and too unsure

I am a woman of my word

Open your ears I'm pretty sure you heard

Heard how good I am

Heard I'm a really good friend

But do not get it twisted I will dismiss, unfriend, and forget if you

ever in your life miss treat this

Cliche but I deserve the world

The last dude couldn't even give me a block

So I blocked kicked pushed him to the curb

The curb he thought all I would need

I am not new to this

You too old and a fool to this

Thought I would fall for this

My heart too big but my needs not small to this

I have to teach you my all to this

But I have no patience just go and keep your little all to this

I can go on forever

But I'm too good so you and I could never be close ever
again like this
My friend, I am not new to this

Nasty

Classy nasty sassy

Hell you asked me

In a rush never hushed

Making moves too much to lose

Attitude so you can never abuse

Stand back

Never a running back

No time

On my grind

Nasty

Talk about me

In a minute I am going to have you asking about me

So real

Nasty

Now what was that you heard about me

Standout

I rather live than die

Go for what I know than be shy

Take it slow cause this world moving at a fast pace

Love who I love anymore can see the door

Take a stand cause too many bowing down

Standout because too many people blending in

Speak my mind cause no one has a voice

Be a leader cause they all follow

Stay positive cause too much negativity

Think before I act cause no one has a brain

Make a change cause everyone wants to remain the same

Latausha Bonner

Most Times

Sometimes you have to lose to win
Sometimes you have to run away to miss
Sometimes you have to go broke to get rich
Sometimes a million no's will turn into one yes
Sometimes you have to fall to get back up
And most times you have to cry to smile again
Sometimes what is blind you can see
Most times what is real is real
What is fake is fake
The person they are showing you is really them
And how they feel they are not hiding that from you
Sometimes what is is and what is not is not
Stop believing you are special and it could have never
happened to you
Or this happened because of that
Or that happened because of this
No, it happened because it was supposed to happen
Sometimes you see the truth
But most times you already knew it was the truth

Reality is not fake and fake is not reality all you have to do is open your eyes. Put to the side how much you like someone. Check that at the door. Sometimes a person will abuse you because they know how much you like them. Stop saying you been played or you were blind. You just did not want to know the truth because we all know the truth hurts.

Different

My heart so different from you all

I actually give a damn

Seem like you not showing the same give a damn

Who I look like Uncle Sam

I see through all the maybes rolling of the eyes and when you hesitate

Well maybe I should have hesitated and taken a moment and meditated

So simple and there is nothing that should be debated

Do You

I am working out to get a better body
That does not mean I want attention
I am going to school to get a career to make more money
That does not mean I owe you anything
I spend a lot of time alone to get my mind right
That does not mean you should take it personally
I think highly of myself and it took a while
But that does not mean I think I am better than you
Point being DO YOU
No matter what he said or she said
DO YOU

People will literally take you wanting to become a better person personal. Mind blowing. I guess they can't help it.

Latausha Bonner

Pause

He still where I left him

Even though it's been so long

Every now and then I do think about him like a slow jam love song

Pause

No, I'm lying

He still where I left him

Broke, mad, and worried looking

He still where I left him

Now I am not worried about a thing

So glad he left

Glad I missed that wedding ring

He still exactly where I left him

No life, low life, high all his life, selfish, and all about his life

Listen he still where I left him

Knew it was not my fault

But the people standing behind him pointing at me like a
brainwashed colt

It's funny because he still where I left him

Too damn grown and I am not the one to pick up no grown

ass man's slack

He knows damn well never in his life to try and come back

PYT

If my sexy offends you I wonder if me telling you what's on my

mind would embarrass you

I offended you

Sorry I offended you

The lips on my face will not stop moving

The ears on my head cannot help but keep listening

These eyes on my face tell from afar you a lie

Why are you so surprised I cannot understand why

I get offended by your offense

Had to take a step back to reminisce

Go to sleep wake back up to re-envision this

On top

Won't stop

Get your life together

Cause I wish I might apologize for any of this

I am the shit

You love me

But you hate to love me

Just a PYT out here doing her thing

And I can't stop

Won't stop any of this

Latausha Bonner

You Better

You think you the best

You better

You think you got the best

Girl you better

Can't no one touch you

Go ahead you better

You got the best hairstyles

Girl you better

No one messing with your love stroke

Come on girl you better

Let them run up on you if they want to

Girl you better

Can't no one touch you or your team

Go head you better

All the men want you

Yes you better

Even the ones never saw you before

I know that's right you better

You are the best

You are on top

No one can think highly of you like you can. Think you are the best because you are. Think no one can touch you because they can't. Think you can get whatever you want because you can. It has nothing to do with being arrogant. You know you and as long as you know no one can play, force, or try to encourage you to be someone else.....

YOU WILL ALWAYS STAY TRUE TO YOU

Your

Truth

Is

Inside

You

Stop Ignoring It

Chapter Five

Be Honest With Yourself

Are you confident in yourself?

Being confident in yourself takes more than just saying it, you have to feel it, live it, and make it rub off on other people. Your glow is proof how confident you are in yourself. The way you speak is proof you're confident in yourself and how you speak about other people is also proof how confident you are in yourself. People can literally feel and see your confidence from afar.

When faced with problems how do you handle them?

This goes back to confidence. When you know you are putting your best foot forward you will go for nothing less. Do you scream, argue, and talk over people? Why can't you get your point across by talking like adults in a calm and understanding manner? I get it hurt people hurt people, but how can your point get across if you are not speaking clear and calm? Different situations cause a different reaction. Because you are confident in yourself you know you are being the best mate you can be, and you want to resolve things before they get out of hand, also you will not make things worse. If the other person does not love you enough to change things that are hurting you then you have to walk away, not because you gave up but because you know you deserve better.

Why are you so afraid to be alone?

There is nothing wrong with being in a relationship, but WHEN YOU ARE READY. Too many people get in relationships hurt, mentally all over the place, still in love with their ex, too much baggage from their last relationship, and/or financially not ready. They bring someone else in their life and wonder why it is not working out. Why not take the time to get to know you first? Why can't you do that for you? What is so special about this other person that they will not wait for you? And you feeling like you have to get them before someone else gets them. Believe me, if someone loves you they will wait for you, no arguing about that. Get your mind right, get to know you, and love yourself first so you can be able to love someone else.

Do you feel you are missing out on love?

There are millions and millions of people in this world, what are you missing out on? People get married at 85 years old, what are you missing out on? If you rush a relationship I am telling you right now you will settle, be angry with yourself, be bitter, and not have that other person's full attention or respect. Why, because you did not get to know that other person or make them invest in you. You have nothing but time, so do not make someone else make you feel like anything has to be rushed or it will be over!

Why are you so soft when it comes to your mate and not hold them accountable for what they did or said they will do?

Too many people are afraid of their mate leaving if they tell them how they feel. Why? If your relationship is not strong enough or your friendship is not strong enough when you express the way you feel they may leave because they are not strong enough to listen to their faults or change because you are hurt. They really do not care about you to understand your feelings. They have other people to tend to and not your nagging self. This is why communication is so important at the beginning of the relationship or friendship. Both of you tell what you expect and what you will not go for at the beginning. This way each other already has an idea of what the other one wants, needs, and what they will not go for. No misunderstandings, no confusion, and not one person being clueless.

Why is it so easy for you to talk about someone else relationship problems but not your own?

It is hard for someone to look in the mirror and realize what is going on in his or her life, but so easy for them to judge someone else situation. Why is it so easy for someone to say what someone else is doing wrong? What someone else has to change to make his or her situation better? But when looking at their own life it is all messed up because they worry about other people's relationship and not their own. Their own relationship is suffering because they refuse to face those problems because they are deep-rooted. They judge other people's relationship because it is easier for them to live with. Judging someone else is easier for them to live with than facing their own problems and dealing with them? WOW! But it is real. Deal with your problems and find your happiness. It's simple!

Latausha Bonner

Why can't you walk away?

Simple question right? You know you can do better, you know you deserve better, you know better is out there, you know you have had better, so what is the problem?

Why is it easier to settle, why is it easier to cry, to worry, to stress, to have bad health from not eating, to get headaches from not sleeping, or getting nothing done from worrying? Is the reason kids, money, or love? Nothing is more important than your happiness. With happiness, other blessings happen, so why when asked "How are you doing" You cannot answer "Happy" with a straight face? How are you doing for real? Why does that other person have such a hold on you? Them being in your life does not equal your happy!

Why can't you speak your mind?

There are so many people in relationships right now who do not speak their mind. Passive aggressiveness is real, and too many people are passive-aggressive, but they do not know it. If a person can walk away while you are having an important conversation with them or expressing the way you feel they do not care about you. If they hear you up all night crying but pretends they do not know they do not care about you, and if a person does not change when you tell them how you feel, they do not respect you. Sometimes look from the outside in. Take a step back from yourself. Look in the mirror and be as honest as you can with yourself. How are you doing? Not how your mate makes you feel, how are you doing?

How do you view YOURSELF?

Look in the mirror right now and tell yourself what do you see. Why do you let the opinions of other people make you see yourself differently? Why can't you see yourself as special and no one else looks like you? You are not weak, but very sure and secure in yourself. Say it now "I am not weak and I am very sure and secure in myself" Talk to yourself every day. Make yourself feel like no one is like you, you deserve the world, you are special, and believe what you say! In return, it will happen and your feelings about yourself will change.

Are you strong enough for a relationship

Many people will say yes to this, but most of them cannot hold a conversation, cannot express themselves when something upsets them, cannot find themselves to care when they hurt someone else, will go to bed mad, will ignore whenever they feel like it, will text instead of call when they don't feel like being bothered, give up when times get hard, are selfish, will not give their mate their last, will not sacrifice once they are in a relationship, and once people get comfortable they do not treat their mate the same. So, again are you ready for a relationship?

No one can be honest with you but you!

Please Remember

The signs are there. People basically tell you to your face how they feel about you.

What they say to you, how they act toward you, how they act when other people are around you, how much time they spend with you, the way they actually talk to you, if they actually call you instead of text you, how they sex you, what money they have to spend on you, how their family members treat you, how they express the way they are feeling about you or what is going on, are all signs of how that person feels about you. Do not ignore the signs, they are right in your face. It is all about what is most important to them. How they respect you and their loyalty and honesty to you.

Pay close attention!

The people you surround yourself with will mold your thinking, your happiness, and outcomes of your relationships. Women are a prize that many men desire, and there are lots of women that need to realize this, so this is what actually got Latausha started with wanting to write this poem book. This poem book was a way to express how Latausha feels about men, the things Latausha thinks women should do, act on, and not do.

Listen, if their love does not add or multiply up to the love you are giving subtract and divide that person out of your life.

And listen your dreams are real. You can see and basically feel them, so why waste any more time or even care how other people feel.

Easier said than done, but please remember...

YOU MATTER

About Author

Latausha Bonner has been writing a very long time. For years she has been writing love, hate, inspirational, break up to make up and relationship poems. The things that trigger Latausha's writings is the things going on around her. She knew what she was always born to do and that was to inspire you to realize your worth and that you are worthy. Latausha was born and raised in Erie Pennsylvania. She went to college online at the University of Phoenix and graduated with an Associates Degree in Arts. At this moment Latausha is working on more inspirational books for women and starting a small book business. For more information about Latausha Bonner please visit her website at HTTP://lataushabonner.wix.com/mysite

"The Core Truth of it all" is powerful, motivational, and the author hopes she has inspired YOU!

Contact The Author

Facebook:www.Facebook.com/lataushabonner

Email:lataushabutterflyb@yahoo.com

lataushabonner2014@gmail.com

Blog: http://lataushabonner.wix.com/mysite

The Core Truth of it all